Arguments for God

Philosophy of Religion Study Guide

Clare Jarmy

First published 2013

by PushMe Press

Mid Somerset House, Southover, Wells, Somerset BA5 1UH

www.pushmepress.com

© 2014 Inducit Learning Ltd

The right of Clare Jarmy to be identified as author of this work has been asserted by her in accordance with sections 77 and 78 of the Copyright, Designs and Patents Act 1988.

All rights reserved. No part of this book may be reprinted or reproduced or utilised in any form or transmitted by any electronic, mechanical, or other means, now known or hereafter invented, including photocopying and recording, or in any information storage or retrieval system, without permission in writing from the publishers.

British Library Cataloguing in Publication Data
A catalogue record for this book is available from the British Library

ISBN: 978-1-909618-36-7 (pbk)
ISBN: 978-1-909618-37-4 (ebk)
ISBN: 978-1-910252-90-1 (hbk)
ISBN: 978-1-910252-91-8 (pdf)

Typeset in Frutiger by booksellerate.com
Printed by Lightning Source

A rich and engaging community assisted by the best teachers in Philosophy

philosophy.pushmepress.com

Students and teachers explore Philosophy of Religion through handouts, film clips, presentations, case studies, extracts, games and academic articles.

Pitched just right, and so much more than a textbook, here is a place to engage with critical reflection whatever your level. Marked student essays are also posted.

Contents

Introduction 7
The Cosmological Argument 19
The Teleological Argument 43
The Ontological Argument 65
The Moral Argument 87
Postscript 115

Introduction

WHAT'S AN ARGUMENT?

In common parlance, the term "argument" has two main meanings. First, it means a disagreement and exchange of views between at least two parties. We often, therefore, see "argument" as an intrinsically negative and divisive thing. Secondly, it is sometimes used in the sense of a persuasive thread that runs through a piece of writing or perhaps a speech (such as "The Prime Minister's argument was that increasing public spending would be irresponsible in the current economic climate").

The word "argument" in everyday speech is almost never used in the sense that we mean it in philosophy. Arguments are quite a formal thing: they are claims, which following logically to lead to a **CONCLUSION**. These arguments are sometimes known as **SYLLOGISMS**, and the claims that form the basis of a philosophical argument are called **PREMISES**.

So, let's look at a good example of a basic argument, or syllogism.

- All philosophers are wise.
- Clare is a philosopher.
- Therefore, Clare is wise.

1 and 2 are premises - they are the two claims from which the conclusion is derived.

VALID AND SOUND ARGUMENTS

Arguments can be good and bad, and we judge them based on what we call their **VALIDITY** and their **SOUNDNESS**. Validity is a measure of whether the argument follows logically to a conclusion. Soundness is a measure of whether the premises are true.

Validity

Let's look back at the argument about how wise I am. We can see it's valid, because if all philosophers are wise and I am one, then it follows that I must be wise. Put another way, a valid argument is one where if the premises are true, the conclusion can't be false. We can therefore tell whether the argument is valid by thinking about all the possible configurations of true and false, and seeing whether the conclusion comes out as true.

Compare that with another example:

- If it's raining, I'll take an umbrella.
- It's not raining.
- Therefore, I won't take an umbrella.

This argument is **INVALID**. It is based on a logical flaw, because there is no claim in the first premise that suggests that **ONLY** if it's raining, will I take an umbrella. Think about it: you might take an umbrella because you think it might rain, or because it's snowing, or because it's really hot and you want to keep off the sun. In other words, **THE CONCLUSION DOESN'T FOLLOW FROM THE PREMISES** in this argument.

Soundness

Now, let's look a bit more into soundness. We've said that the argument about philosophers' wisdom is valid, but is it sound? Remember, that the soundness of arguments is all about whether the premises are true, so we need to look at the claims being made in the argument. Firstly, are all philosophers wise? Well, from Socrates' point of view, all philosophers are, almost by definition, wise. This is because they are the only people who escape "the cave" that is normal human understanding, which he sees to be very limited. However this might not be persuasive in that Socrates' definition of a true "philosopher" might only apply to a very select few, leaving out people we might consider to be philosophers.

The argument begs the question: what is a philosopher? If a philosopher is anyone who has done a philosophy degree, then it seems that they are not likely all to be wise. If, on the hand, they are people who live as Socrates taught, perhaps they are? This calls into question the second premise - "Clare is a philosopher" - because I am a philosopher in the sense that I did a philosophy degree, but I don't live very successfully by Socrates' teachings, so I'm not a philosopher by that definition.

That's all been quite involved, and we haven't even looked into how to define the term "wise". You can see that validity is quite clear-cut, but soundness is not always easy to establish. Soundness is also something about which **THERE COULD BE DEBATE** in the sense that some people might think that a certain premise is true, and others might think it's false. Validity is not to be debated - something either logically follows or it does not.

Just to complicate matters, an argument **CAN BE VALID BUT NOT SOUND**. Take the following example:

- All flibs are swarls.
- Some flibs are geigh.
- Therefore, some swarls are geigh.

This argument is valid - you can see that the logic follows. However, the argument is not sound because not one of the things mentioned is real.

An argument **CANNOT BE SOUND BUT INVALID**, because even if its premises are true, without validity, an argument is pointless. So, for example:

- Socks are worn on the feet.
- Feet are below the knees.
- Therefore, Friday comes after Thursday.

The premises and the conclusion are true, but we wouldn't call the argument sound, because it doesn't hang together logically.

TYPES OF ARGUMENT

Before we turn to argument for the existence of God, we need to know about two different types of argument: **INDUCTIVE** and **DEDUCTIVE** arguments.

Simply put, **INDUCTIVE** arguments take their premises from **THE WORLD**, and use logic to draw a conclusion about a matter of fact. For example:

- When there are dark clouds in the sky, it is likely to rain.
- Today, there are dark clouds in the sky.
- Therefore, it is likely to rain.

The logic used in these kinds of argument is **A POSTERIORI**, which means "that coming afterwards" - it is logic based on experience.

DEDUCTIVE arguments often have **DEFINITIONS** or **INESCAPABLE TRUTHS** as premises; premises that need not be experienced, for example:

- All bachelors are unmarried men.
- David is a bachelor.
- Therefore, he is unmarried.

We don't need to go and ask David if he is married, because by definition, being a bachelor, he must be unmarried. So we can see that this kind of argument **REQUIRES NO EXPERIENCE** in establishing its soundness. The kind of reasoning used here is **A PRIORI** - which means "from something before". In other words, it is based on knowledge we have already, for which no experience is required to undertake this kind of reasoning.

Deductive arguments are stronger than inductive arguments.

When an argument is based on definitions, if it is valid and sound, the conclusion is established unequivocally. Inductive arguments are usually seen to be weaker, because there is always debate to be had about whether an inductive premise, one discovered through experience, is true or not.

However, because deductive arguments have to be based on definitions, and premises that don't require experience, **THEY OFTEN DON'T TELL US MUCH THAT IS NEW**. The conclusions to deductive arguments are often seen to be obvious. The bachelor argument above is a good example. All that needs to be said is that David is a bachelor for us to know he must be unmarried. This is both why the argument is strong, and also why it is not that interesting.

So, now we have examined in detail what an argument is, how we measure its validity and soundness, and what types of arguments there are. We can now, therefore move on to discuss arguments for the existence of God.

ARGUMENTS FOR THE EXISTENCE OF GOD

Now we move on from talking about arguments in general to our specific topic - arguments for the existence of God. The arguments for the existence of God are interesting for a number of ways.

Firstly, they are interesting because they largely formalise and defend the evidence that religious believers have always cited for belief in God. There are wonderings that all humans must have at some point:

- "How did this all get here?"
- "The world's so perfectly set up: can it be chance?"
- "What would implications of the idea of the greatest conceivable being be?"
- "Where did morality come from?"

These questions are the starting point from whence the four arguments we are going to examine begin. This makes the arguments **INTUITIVE**, which is to say that they are in line with common human experience of the world.

Secondly, arguments for the existence of God are interesting because although believers might see them as persuasive, **IT IS RELATIVELY RARE THAT SOMEONE COMES TO BELIEF IN GOD THROUGH EXAMINING ONE OF THESE ARGUMENTS**. More frequently, it seems that assenting to a belief in the existence of God is a matter of faith and practice, rather than a matter of undergoing a process of philosophical enquiry. As Anselm puts it, this is "faith seeking understanding". The purpose might be to underline faith, not to create it.

Thirdly, these arguments are interesting because different groups of religious believers will disagree about their relative importance. In the Roman Catholic tradition, and more catholic traditions in the Church of England, there has, historically been a tendency to place great emphasis on the role of human reason. It is believed that reason is a God-given faculty, and that, therefore, it has a role to play in faith. **THOMAS AQUINAS** (1225-1274), one of the most important theologians of all time, argued that, as there is only one truth (whereby a claim is either true or false), faith and reason must ultimately coincide, and hence where there seems to be conflict between the truths of faith and the truths of reason, no real conflict must ultimately be there.

So to this point of view, arguments for the existence of God are important, because human reason is understood to be a good way of comprehending the world and the divine.

On the other side, there are the Protestants, by which we mean Lutherans, Calvinists, Baptists, Methodists as well as numerous other groups. Protestantism was epitomised by the man usually seen to be its founder, Martin Luther (1483-1546), in the sentiment that we are "justified by faith" - that the relationship between God and humankind was most important, and that the individual's faith, not his reason, is the thing that will save him.

This promotion of faith as the ideal takes another giant step away from the view that reason governs all in the writings of **SOREN KIRKEGAARD** (1813-1855), when in the book *Fear and Trembling*, he promotes the "leap of faith" as being more holy than obeying the dictates of reason. He use the example of Abraham, who obeyed when God asked him to sacrifice his son, the most unreasonable and unfathomable request that could have been made. Kirkegaard claims that Abraham is the epitome of what Christianity should promote as religious devotion, and thereby puts reason right to the bottom of the pile, with faith ruling supreme.

So, it's fair to say that not all religious believers agree on the role that reason, and by extension arguments for the existence of God have in religious belief.

However, these arguments have a power that has led to philosophers formulating and reformulating them throughout the centuries. Many of them have a long history - often dating back to medieval or ancient Greek philosophy - but they don't start and end there. All four arguments are still commented on, discussed and developed at the highest levels in the discipline of the Philosophy of Religion, even to this day.

There is something about these arguments that means people never seem to lose interest in thinking through and tackling them anew. We said at the beginning that these arguments draw on core questions in human experience; perhaps that's why they are still so much discussed hundreds of years after most of them were first formulated.

KEY TERMS

- **A POSTERIORI** - Literally "that coming afterwards", a posteriori reasoning is that which uses evidence from the world around us.

- **A PRIORI** - Literally "from something before", a priori reasoning is that which uses no evidence from the world, rather it is based on the workings of logic and definitions.

- **ARGUMENT** - When used as a philosophical term, an argument is a logical progression of ideas towards a conclusion.

- **CONCLUSION** - The final element in a philosophical argument, it is the statement which is asserted as being true as a result of the evidence given in the argument.

- **DEDUCTIVE** - An argument that deduces a conclusion based on reasoning a priori.

- **INDUCTIVE** - An argument that derives its conclusion based on reasoning a posteriori.

- **INVALID** - An argument where the premises do not follow infallibly to the conclusion.

- **PREMISE** - A statement that is used as evidence in a philosophical argument.

- **SOUND** - An argument where the premises are true.

- **SYLLOGISM** - A name given to philosophical arguments where premises lead logically to a conclusion.

- **VALID** - An argument where the conclusion follows from the premises - where it would be impossible for the premises to be true and the conclusion false.

SELF-ASSESSMENT QUESTIONS

- What is the difference between how the term "argument" is used in common parlance, and how it is used by philosophers?

- Give an example of an inductive premise.

- Give an example of a deductive premise.

- In what way might it be said that deductive arguments are more effective than inductive arguments?

- In what way might you argue that inductive arguments are more effective than deductive arguments?

- Your friend accuses you of giving an invalid argument - what is she claiming is wrong with your argument?

- Give an example of an argument that is valid but not sound.

- What role do arguments for the existence of God tend to have in people's faith?

- How is the standard Roman Catholic approach to arguments for the existence of God best summarised?

- How does a Protestant approach differ from this?

FURTHER READING

- **COLE, P** - Philosophy of Religion, Hodder Education, (a number of editions available) Chapters 1 and 9

- **PHELAN, J** - Philosophy: Themes and Thinkers, CUP, Appendix 2

- **SOLOMON, R** - Introducing Philosophy, OUP, Introduction, Section D

The Cosmological Argument

The first argument that we shall examine is an **INDUCTIVE ARGUMENT** for God's existence, which as we learned in the introduction means its premises are drawn from the world around us. That is to say that it has an **EMPIRICAL** element to it - it looks to **EVIDENCE** based on what we perceive.

The name for this argument comes from two Ancient Greek words "kosmos", which means "universe" and "logo", which has a large number of meanings, but which here is probably best translated "logic" or "reasoning". The cosmological argument is therefore "reasoning on the universe". This is an argument that draws evidence for the existence of God based on the existence and nature of the universe itself. Often called the "first cause argument", the cosmological argument plays on the common questions asked by humankind since time immemorial such as "how did we get here?" and "why is there something, rather than nothing?"

ST THOMAS AQUINAS (1225-1274)

The person most commonly associated with the cosmological argument is the 13th-C thinker St Thomas Aquinas, an Italian Dominican Monk whose scholarly output was so extraordinary, both in terms of its scope and its depth, that his influence on the philosophy of religion and Roman Catholic theology is still much in evidence to this day. For many, he is an embodiment of the philosophy of the medieval period.

Given that Aquinas lived for only 49 years, the sheer amount he wrote is particularly impressive. He is thought to have composed around 60 works in his short lifetime. He achieved this great feat by dictating different books to several scribes, all at the same time. This example goes to show the enormous power of this man's mind, that he could compose books on totally different subjects concurrently.

Aquinas is synonymous in many people's minds with a movement called Scholasticism. Scholasticism emerged because of one extraordinary event - the collection and translation into Latin of all of Aristotle's works. This was happening in the late twelfth and early thirteenth centuries, and it brought a new, Aristotelian, way of looking at the world, particularly amongst scholars at the University of Paris, which was a great seat of learning at the time. Of all of these 13th-C philosophers, the Scholastics, Aquinas is by far the best known.

So Aquinas was a thinker greatly influenced by Aristotle. This approach was initially very controversial because Aristotle lived before Jesus, so some authorities within The Church saw it as setting up a pagan philosopher as an authority on Christian teaching, rather than relying on early church fathers such as Augustine. But Aquinas was a great synthesiser, believing there to be one truth, but many relevant sources. Still, Aquinas often refers to Aristotle simply as "the philosopher", which indicates the centrality of Aristotelian thinking in Aquinas' work.

But Aquinas' work is doing much more than providing footnotes on Aristotle. Aquinas in all his works is performing a careful balancing act, trying to interpret the teachings of the Church with the philosophical method and approach of Aristotle. If you go to the National Gallery in London, you can see there the Demidoff Altarpiece, on which there is a depiction of Aquinas holding in one hand, the Church, and in the other, a book. Although the content of the book in the depiction is not decipherable, many have taken this to symbolise Aquinas' mission to show the teachings of Aristotle in the light of Christian revelation, and vice versa.

The upshot of all of this is that it is impossible to understand Aquinas in isolation - we will inevitably end up talking about some of Aristotle's ideas as well.

Aquinas' Cosmological Arguments

So now we have looked at Aquinas' general approach, we can get onto his cosmological argument, or, as I should say, arguments, because he actually gives three.

These three arguments are found in the Summa Theologiae (Collected Theology), and are the first three of Aquinas' so-called "Five ways" (Quinque Viae); five logical routes to belief in God. Aquinas calls them "proofs" because he believes that the existence of God is not self-evident (we will see why he thinks this in the chapter on the ontological argument). Aquinas believed that the existence of God should be demonstrated logically and rationally, using evidence.

Two of the cosmological arguments are quite similar, and one is a little different. They are all cosmological arguments because they deal with the question of how the universe is adequately explained, but as Stephen P Menn notes in The Cambridge Companion to Medieval Philosophy, the first two of Aquinas' cosmological arguments are based on physical phenomena that we see around us, and the third is based on the kind of existence that the universe has, and how God's existence is different.

Way 1 - motion and change

Aquinas called his first argument the "most manifest"; he thought this was his most obvious argument, perhaps because it sticks so closely to what Aristotle says in his books Physics and Metaphysics. It is clear that Aquinas is using Aristotle's ideas about motion and change and reconciling them with Christian teachings (c.f. Aristotle Physics VIII - 4-5; Metaphysics XII).

Aquinas' First Way (paraphrased for clarity)

1. In the world some things move and change.

2. Whatever moves or changes is moved or changed by another - it cannot move or change without outside input.

3. It is therefore impossible that a thing could move or change by itself.

4. Therefore, whatever is in motion must be put in motion by another (mini conclusion).

5. If the thing that causes movement or change is also moved or changed, then this also must be moved or changed by something else, and so on - we get a chain of movement/change.

6. But this cannot go on to infinity, because then there would be no first mover, and so the movement or change would have never started in the first place.

7. Therefore it is necessary to arrive at a first mover, which is moved or changed by nothing; and "this everyone understands to be God" (main conclusion).

We can see that this argument is more complex than the arguments we looked at in the introduction, because there are **TWO CONCLUSIONS** - there's an argument in premises 1-3, and a mini conclusion (called an **INTERMEDIATE CONCLUSION** by philosophers), and from this mini-conclusion, another argument follows, and we finally reach our **MAIN CONCLUSION**.

So, how has Aquinas logically argued from the presence of motion and change in the world to the existence of God? An example often given here is that of a row of dominos. Imagine a row of dominos lined up in a room. Now, imagine that this is a room where there is going to be no movement or change - no wind, no-one going in there, no doors slamming - nothing apart from the conditions, as they are, inside that room full of dominos, lined up.

Will the dominos topple? We know that rows of dominos have the potential to topple, but in this movement and change-free room, the dominos never will topple. The reason for this is that although we know rows of dominos can topple - they have that potential - they never will until something moves the first one. This is what Aquinas means when he claims that something can't cause itself to move or change. It has to be moved or change by something else.

Now imagine that the row of dominos is set out in a series of many rooms, going through door after door. You are at the end, but you can't see another end. Suddenly, you hear a clatter in one of the other rooms, and after a while, the clattering sound gets closer, until the dominos in the room you are standing in start to topple over, one by one but quickly, until all the dominoes you can see have toppled over. What assumption do you make about how your dominos toppled over? Which of these two propositions do you think is more likely?

23

1. The first domino, that you couldn't see, was moved, and this caused the movement in the rest of the row of dominos, which ultimately caused the last domino in the room you were standing in to fall over.

2. There is an infinite number of dominos, so the movement in the row of dominos had no beginning.

You would, almost certainly, assume that a) was true, and b) was false. Why? Because proposition b) fails to demonstrate how the movement started, and hence fails to demonstrate how the final domino fell over. Proposition a), on the other hand, can explain the movement of the last domino, because of the movement of the first domino. This is why Aquinas rejects the idea that movement or change regresses infinitely - because then the movement would have never started. This is incredibly important; the whole argument hinges on this point.

So, given Aquinas has rejected the possibility of an infinite regression of movement or change, it follows that there has to be a first mover, an unmoved-mover, which itself is unmoved and unchanged, but which is the origin of movement and change in everything else. This is, as Aquinas says, what "everyone understands to be God".

▸ **Way 2**

The second of Aquinas' arguments seems familiar for two reasons. Firstly, he uses the same pattern of reasoning in Way 2 as Way 1, replacing the idea of "move/change" with "cause". But the other reason it might seem familiar, if you have covered this in your course, is that it sounds like Aristotle's argument for the Prime Mover - the ultimate explanation of the universe. There are many similarities with Aristotle's ideas to be found in Ways 1 and 2 as we have said, but there is a crucial difference. Aristotle explains that the Prime Mover is a final cause, that is to say, the purpose of the universe. Aquinas on the other hand is talking about God as an efficient cause: a causal explanation for the existence of the universe. His argument goes as follows:

Aquinas' Second Way (paraphrased for clarity)

1. In the world, we find chains of cause and effect - every effect has a cause, which is itself caused.

2. It would be impossible that thing is found to be the cause of itself; because then it would have had to exist before it existed, which is impossible.

3. It is not possible for chains of cause and effect to go back infinitely, because then nothing would have ever been caused - to remove the first cause it to remove the last cause.

4. Therefore, if there is no first cause, there will be no last effect, which is plainly not the case because the world is full of things that are effects of causes.

5. Therefore it is necessary to admit a first efficient cause, to which everyone gives the name of God.

In Way 2, Aquinas moves beyond the argument that has come before in Way 1. Aquinas is no longer trying to explain phenomena within the universe, but the existence of the universe itself. By looking at a simple example, we can see how his argument works.

Bertie works in an office. A rumour is making its way round his co-workers that he is having an affair with Martha, who works on the desk nearest his. Imagine you were new to working in that office, and you heard the rumour - you would assume that either there was something to it, and Bertie was seeing Martha, or you would think that someone had made it up. Whether or not the rumour's true, it must have an **ORIGIN**. Now, imagine someone said to you "no, that rumour has always been going around; it had no beginning". You wouldn't believe them. Why? Because if there was no first person spreading the rumour, the rumour wouldn't have spread. Without the first uttering of it, there is no last utterance of it.

Aquinas says that the universe is like this. As everything has a cause, and these things are caused, and those causes have causes and so on, that suggests that there has to be a first cause. Why can't these causes regress ad infinitum? Because if there were no beginning to the chain of cause and effect, there would be no last effect in the chain. So, if there were no beginning to the universe, nothing else would be here now. It seems from Aquinas' reasoning that there must be a first cause, and this is, as he says, what "everyone understands to be God".

Following the same path, but possibly from a different angle, is **THE KALAM ARGUMENT**, which was formulated by Islamic philosophers who were also influenced by Aristotle, at roughly the same time that Aquinas was writing. The attention the argument has received recently has been largely due to the work of William Lane Craig, a Roman Catholic philosopher who formulates it thus:

The Kalam Argument (as formulated by William Lane Craig)

- All things that had a beginning had a cause.

- The universe had a beginning.

- Therefore, the universe had a cause: God.

This argument is noticeably simpler than Aquinas' argument, and relies on premises that Lane Craig would argue are extremely intuitive. It seems obvious to us that having a beginning implies being caused.

For example, this afternoon, my television switched on without my turning it on. I did not respond that it must have just done this without a cause. I checked I had not sat on the remote control. I checked that there was not a programme I had put on the timer to watch. I wondered if one of the other electrical devices in the room was somehow interfering with the signal. I wondered if someone was using a remote control next door. A person with a certain mindset might attribute its randomly switching on to a poltergeist (though this explanation would not, I have to say, occur to me). The point is that when something happens, we do not think it has no cause, and so the first premise of the Kalam argument seems very strong.

Notice that if we accept premise 1, then all we have to do is agree to the premise that the universe had a beginning, for the argument to seem broadly valid. We will speak later about whether the universe could conceivably have had no beginning.

▸ Way 3

The third of Aquinas' cosmological arguments takes a different tack, focusing as we said earlier on the nature of God, rather than a physical, almost mechanistic explanation of the universe. It is seen by some, including Fr Robert Barron, to be the most fundamental of the five ways in terms of summing up Aquinas' understanding of the nature of God.

In order to understand this argument, we need first to go through two commonly used philosophical concepts - those of **CONTINGENCY** and **NECESSITY**.

Contingency is all about **POSSIBILITY**. If it rains tomorrow, the fact of it raining is a contingent fact because it could have not rained - rain was one of the possibilities. Necessity on the other hand is about **ALWAYS** or **NEVER**. Some days it will rain, and some days it will not, but 2+2=4 will always be true, and 2+2=5 will always be false. They are different sorts of claims to the claims about rain.

We can also talk of contingent and necessary being. You are a contingent being - you came into existence, you will (sadly) go out of existence one day, and you might never have existed at all. You, and I and everyone one and everything in the universe is a "might not have been" - everything is contingent (dependent) on something else for its existence.

A necessary being would be of an utterly different kind, unlike us and everything else in the universe. A necessary being is one that **COULD NOT NOT EXIST**.

CONTINGENT	NECESSARY
Possible - might be, might not be	Always true or impossible - always false
Dependent	Independent
Could come into existence	Could never come into existence
Could go out of existence	Could never go out of existence

So, there are two realms: the contingent and the necessary. Aquinas is going to argue for the existence of a necessary being, on the basis of the contingent beings in the universe. Let's now see how he goes about it.

Aquinas' Third Way (paraphrased for clarity)

1. We find in nature things that are possible to be and not to be. They come into and go out of existence, and consequently, they are possible to be and not to be.

2. These things cannot have always existed, because these things have to come into existence - at some time, they didn't exist.

   - Therefore, if everything in the world has to come into existence, then at one time there must have been nothing in existence.

3. Now if this were true, there would be nothing in existence now, because something can only be brought into existence by something that exists.

4. Therefore, if at one time nothing was in existence, it would have been impossible for anything to have begun to exist; and thus even now nothing would be in existence - which is absurd.

   - Therefore, not all beings are merely possible, but there must exist something the existence of which is necessary. This all men speak of as God.

The argument works on a truth we all acknowledge - that we come into existence, go out of existence and do not hold within ourselves a sufficient explanation for our existence.

How does Aquinas get from the fleetingness of life to the existence of God? Perhaps as long as there is another contingent being that goes before any other contingent being, we don't need a necessary being? In other words, could we not deny Aquinas' intermediate conclusion?

Peter Kreeft formulated an example that we could use here to explain why Aquinas thought that a **DIFFERENT KIND OF BEING** was needed to account for the existence of contingent beings. Imagine there's a book you really want to read. Your friend says she'll lend it to you. You ask if she has the book. She replies that she needs to borrow it from a friend. You ask if he has the book. She says that he needs to borrow it from a library. You ask if the library has the book, and she says that they don't have it - they need to borrow it from another library. You are pretty frustrated, and ask who actually has the book. Your friend replies that no one has the book; it is just borrowed. You would think that this was an unsatisfactory answer, **BECAUSE IF THERE IS ONLY BORROWING, AND NO ONE ACTUALLY HAS THE BOOK, THEN THERE IS ACTUALLY NO BORROWING EITHER**. Borrowing only happens when there is at least one owner.

You can see how this relates to Aquinas' argument. If you say that a universe of contingent beings is sufficient explanation for the existence of everything, perhaps you are making the same mistake as the friend who said the book is always borrowed and never owned. **BORROWING REQUIRES AN OWNER**. Perhaps contingency requires necessity, and hence if we agree that the universe and everything in it is contingent, that requires a necessary being.

Necessary Being

It is worth taking a moment to talk about necessary being now, because people tend to get a funny idea about what it means. Often, the idea of a necessary being is depicted as a being that has to exist, and doesn't come into existence or go out of existence.

None of these things is false, but at the same time, it doesn't accurately get the idea across either. If you have the idea of a being that cannot not exist, it sounds like any other being, except with a convenient property of being necessary, which means it does not need the kind of explanation that the universe needs. Seen this way, the idea of a necessary being seems like a cop-out.

However, the idea of a necessary being is much better thought-out than that, and it is certainly not a convenient category of existence dreamed up to get philosophers out of a tricky corner. The idea of necessary existence is the idea of a totally different mode of being.

Many will say that the confusion about necessary being comes when you think of God as a "thing", namely something within the universe that could not not exist. However, the view commonly held by theologians is that God is not a being, but **BEING ITSELF**. We will look later at some of the questions this idea raises.

Sufficient Reason

Some of the common threads that we find in the cosmological arguments, especially in ways 2 and 3 are picked up on by Gottfried Wilhelm Leibniz in his **PRINCIPLE OF SUFFICIENT REASON**. Leibniz coined the phrase, but he is not the only, nor the first exponent of such a view. By "sufficient reason", he means that for any contingent state of affairs, an adequate explanation is needed. If I ask how you come to be reading this, you picking up and looking at the book is an explanation, but it isn't a sufficient reason - it doesn't fully explain how you come to be reading this.

Leibniz used the example of a book of geometry. Say you have a 7th edition of a book of Euclidian geometry, and you want to explain the origin of the material contained within the book. You could say that the 6th edition of the book was an explanation of the material contained within the 7th edition, but although this would provide **AN** explanation, it would not provide a **SUFFICIENT** explanation. The only way to properly account for the material within the book is to look to Euclid, the originator of the material contained within the book. Until we reach Euclid himself, we have not given a **SUFFICIENT REASON** for the book's existence.

Frederick Copleston

In the 20th C, Frederick Copleston was by far the most famous exponent of a modern formulation of the cosmological argument. A Jesuit priest and scholar, Copleston is probably most famous for his extensive series of books on the History of Philosophy. His argument follows Aquinas' third way quite closely in that Copleston's argument too relies on the distinctions of contingent and necessary existence. Copleston interestingly claims that when he talks of God as being "prior" to the existence of the world, he is not meaning simply "before", but he is talking of **ONTOLOGICAL PRIORITY** - that is to say that his argument sets God up not merely as something that came before the universe, but as a being whose existence is on an entirely other level of being from our own.

▸ **Frederick Copleston's argument**

1. There are objects in the universe that are contingent, that is to say that they do not hold within themselves the reason for their existence.

2. Everything in the universe is contingent.

3. The universe is therefore contingent.

4. The universe therefore does not hold within itself the reason for its existence.

5. There must be a reason for existence that exists outside the universe, because nothing within the universe can provide that explanation.

6. "So, I should say, in order to explain existence, we must come to a being which contains within itself the reason for its own existence, that is to say, which cannot not exist".

The 1948 Radio Debate

In 1948, a famous debate was held on the radio between Frederick Copleston and Bertrand Russell, a celebrated philosopher of maths, logician, and writer on all matters philosophical. Like Copleston, Russell is probably best known outside the world of philosophy for his historical work - his History of Western Philosophy is still seen as a key text to this day. Russell was agnostic, and in this debate, Russell offers a searing critique of Copleston's cosmological argument.

Let's summarise the main points made in the debate:

COPLESTON	RUSSELL
The universe is contingent and hence is not explicable by itself. It needs an explanation exterior to it to fully explain it. A Necessary being is needed.	"Necessary" is a term that can only be properly applied to propositions - that is to say that statements that are true by definition. God's existence, were he to exist at all, would be a truth of fact, not a truth of reason.
But you agree that "if there is a contingent being, there is a necessary being" is a necessary statement, don't you?	The ideas of necessary and contingent beings are only coherent "within a logic that I reject"
But doesn't your position lead you to have to deny what seems obvious - that we, and everything in the world relies on something else for our existence - we don't explain our own existence. Now, given that everything in the universe is contingent, there must be something on which they are contingent, namely a necessary being.	Existence cannot be necessary. Take the example of "the existent round square" - by definition, it must exist, because it is existent, but a round square does not exist. Existence cannot be established by definition. There cannot be something whose essence is to exist
So you are forced to stop looking for causes - is it not important to answer the question with a sufficient explanation, not merely some cause but the cause behind the universe?	"Every man who exists has a mother, and it seems to me your argument is that therefore the human race must have a mother, but obviously the human race hasn't a mother -- that's a different logical sphere."
But your solution fails to adequately explain the existence of the universe at all - it is inconceivable that the universe should have no cause at all.	"The physicists assure us that individual quantum transitions in atoms have no cause." "I should say that the universe is just there, and that's all". The universe is a "brute fact".

Is the cosmological argument persuasive?

The most obvious criticism to lay at the door of the cosmological argument is to ask - why must there be a cause external to the universe?

Firstly, some people do not see a problem with the idea of an infinite regress of causes. You could argue that in a causal chain, as long as there is a cause for every effect, then we do not need to ask for a first cause. In other words, we can disagree with Leibniz that only a first cause provides a sufficient reason. As long as each effect has a cause, perhaps that's all we need to ask. Moreover, just because it feels as though the universe ought to have a beginning (after all, we have no experience of anything without a beginning), it does not follow that there could not be a regress in the chain of causes and effects that has no beginning - it does not feel intuitive to us, because we have no experience of anything like that, but that is not the same as saying it is impossible.

Secondly, wouldn't the Big Bang be a sufficient reason to explain the existence of the universe? Supporters of the Big Bang theory, by far the most scientifically credible theory going, will claim that the universe started with a dense "point of singularity" which contained every atom and all energy present in the universe to this day, this point of singularity exploded, and very gradually and in a number of stages, the universe as we know it came about. The evidence for this view comes from the gradual cooling of the universe, as well as the gradual expansion of it. Scientists are therefore able to calculate that the universe is expanding from a single point, and that at some time, the whole universe was present in one point.

William of Ockham (1287-1347) supported the view that "causes must not be multiplied unnecessarily", in a principle that has come to be known as **OCKHAM'S RAZOR**; Ockham encourages us to shave away any explanations that are unnecessary. Perhaps the Big Bang removes the need for God as a first cause?

Does this overcome the need for a first cause? Many will claim that is does, but neither Aquinas nor Copleston would see this as a sufficient explanation to the universe. Copleston would argue that the Big Bang is merely another instance of the same kind of thing as everything else in the universe (a contingent event) the sort of thing that could have not been (the definition of a contingent event, not a necessary one). Therefore Copleston's cosmological argument as well as Aquinas' third way would reject the Big Bang as an explanation for the universe.

But, as Russell correctly noted in his debate with Copleston, quantum physics might show that something can pop into existence with no cause. If this were so, Aquinas' key assumption that **EX NIHILO, NIHILO FIT** (out of nothing comes nothing) would have been shown to be incorrect. If something can some from nothing, then why jump to a God as the explanation for the existence of the universe?

As a counter-argument to Russell, Copleston correctly contests that it is only in very specific circumstances that something on the quantum level can be shown to seemingly pop into existence. This is not the same as demonstrating that a whole universe could come from nothing; implying that all matter in the whole universe, everything that is, comes from nothing. This is quite a jump. However, it is true that it has been shown that the assertion that "nothing can come from nothing" is false.

You could say that the very idea of asking what happened before the Big Bang is incoherent, because modern physics claims that not just matter, but space and time came into existence at this moment. Asking what happened before the Big Bang could therefore be seen as asking what happened in the moments before time existed. This seems like a silly question as there was no time before time existed. How could anything be caused before time existed?

Other critics argue that the cosmological argument contradicts itself. It starts from the premise that everything needs a cause, but ends up concluding exactly the opposite: there is an uncaused cause. If everything needs a cause, then why does God get to be different?

However, Aquinas and Copleston would contest that to suggest God needs a cause would be contrary to what it means to be God. A God that needs a cause is not a God, and hence to suggest that God needs a cause misses the point, rather. God's essence, as Aquinas maintains, is existence, so to suggest God needs a cause is to deny the essential nature of God.

This reply would not convince Russell, who claimed that nothing exists by necessity; to say it can is effectively defining something into existence. I can define something as "the necessarily existent unicorn", yet this doesn't make it pop into existence because I have defined it as existing. However, if we are to accept Russell's argument, we are faced with having to accept that "the universe is just there, and that is all".

Leibniz would not think that this solution is enough. To say the universe is "just there" doesn't even offer a reason for the existence of the universe, let alone a sufficient reason for its existence. Russell's point seems to be dodging the question entirely: it hardly seems as though Russell is playing the game as he has not refuted the argument. He has merely avoided the question.

It seems that we are, then, left at an impasse. There seem to be two choices open to us: to accept the universe as a brute fact, which seems to contradict the principle of sufficient reason, or to accept the existence of a necessary being, which seems to commit a category error by attempting to define something into existence.

Perhaps the term "being" is leading us down a blind alley here. If we look back to what we mean by a necessary being, one that is "being-unqualified" as we examined earlier, God does not need to be a "thing", a "being", but is rather the existence on which and from which everything else is derived. God is that in which we "live and move and have our being" (Acts 17:28), not a magic "thing" outside the universe. Philosophers such as **KEITH WARD** have held this view, and moreover, have pointed out that it seems also to be Aquinas' view.

Blaise Pascal might have felt that this God, the God of Aquinas, was far removed from what he meant by God. When he was 31, he had a vision where he perceived what he claimed to be a truer understanding of the Divine:

> *God of Abraham, God of Isaac, God of Jacob,*
> *Not of the philosophers and scholars.*

The idea of God as "being-unqualified" or "being-itself" is far less problematic to the cosmological argument than the idea of a thing that conveniently cannot not exist, but it seems far removed from the God of devotion and practice; the God of Abraham, God of Isaac and the God of Jacob.

KEY TERMS

- **AD INFINITUM** - Latin: To infinity; infinitely.

- **CONTINGENT BEING** - Dependent on something else for its existence.

- **COSMOLOGICAL** - From Greek - Kosmos and Logos, meaning "reasoning about the universe".

- **EFFICIENT CAUSE** - One of Aristotle's four causes, the efficient cause is the being that brought something about. Aquinas says that a first efficient cause is needed to explain the universe sufficiently.

- **EMPIRICAL** - Based on sensory evidence taken from the world around.

- **EX NIHILO, NIHILO FIT** - Latin: Out of nothing, comes nothing (Aquinas).

- **FINAL CAUSE** - One of Aristotle's four causes, the final cause is the purpose of something. Aristotle claimed God was not a first efficient cause, but was a final cause - the purpose behind the universe.

- **FIRST CAUSE** - Another term for the cosmological argument, this reflects the fact that all cosmological arguments argue for God as the starting point and sufficient explanation for the universe.

- **FIVE WAYS** - The five arguments for the existence of God that Aquinas gives in the Summa Theologiae.

- **INFINITE REGRESS** - Something that goes back infinitely, ie a series with no beginning.

- **KALAM** - A tradition in Islamic philosophy in the Middle Ages, out of which came one formulation of the cosmological argument.

- **NECESSARY BEING** - A being that must exist; one that cannot not exist, which exists independently from anything else, and on which everything else depends.

- **OCKHAM'S RAZOR** - "Do not multiply causes unnecessarily."

- **PRINCIPLE OF SUFFICIENT REASON** - Leibniz' maxim that everything needs not merely an explanation but a sufficient explanation.

- **SCHOLASTICISM** - A tradition in medieval philosophy originating in the fact that Aristotle was newly translated into Latin, and hence became a source for scholars.

SELF-ASSESSMENT QUESTIONS

- What do all cosmological arguments have in common?

- Why does Aquinas reject the possibility of an infinite regress?

- Why does Aquinas argue for a necessary being?

- How is Leibniz' approach to the issue different to Aquinas' cosmological arguments?

- What are the main similarities and differences between Aquinas and Copleston's arguments from contingency and necessity?

- Why could it be argued that the Big Bang does not remove the need for God as a fist cause?

- For what reasons could you reject the whole idea of a necessary being?

- For what reasons might you defend the idea of a necessary being?

- What were the strongest of Russell's arguments in the radio debate, and why?

- How might you defend Copleston against Russell?

FURTHER READING

- **COLE, P** - Philosophy of Religion, Hodder Education, (a number of editions available) Chapter 4

- **DAVIES, B** - An Introduction to The Philosophy of Religion, OUP, Chapter 3

- **JORDAN, LOCKYER AND TATE** - Philosophy of Religion for A level, Nelson Thornes (available in a number of different editions), Chapter 5

- **VARDY, P** - The Puzzle of God, Harper Collins, Chapter 7

The Teleological Argument

The teleological argument is another argument that takes premises from the world of experience. That is to say that it is another **INDUCTIVE** argument for the existence of God, using **A POSTERIORI** reasoning, ie evidence from the senses. The term **TELEOLOGICAL** derives from two Ancient Greek words **TELOS** and **LOGOS**. Logos, as we saw in the chapter on the cosmological argument is best translated "reasoning", and **TELOS** is best translated "goal" or "purpose". So, teleological arguments are **REASONING BASED ON PURPOSE**. The teleological argument takes as its basis the fact that the world seems too purposive or regular to be the result of chance. This is perhaps the most intuitive of the arguments for God, and yet is also one of the most stridently criticised, as we will see later.

Before we go on, it's worth mentioning that you may see this argument referred to as **THE ARGUMENT FROM DESIGN** or **THE DESIGN ARGUMENT** as well as the teleological argument. Without getting too technical, it is largely possible to treat these terms completely interchangeably, and for the purposes of A level, it is certainly possible to do this.

THE ARGUMENT

Teleological arguments are not new by any means, and indeed Ancient Greek thinkers such as Anaxagoras and Empedocles were arguing in this vein even before Socrates was thought of. However, over the course of history, some thinkers' arguments have, rightly or wrongly, been afforded more prominence. Let us begin by looking at the bare bones of what a teleological argument consists of. We can then look in more detail at specific teleological arguments formulated by philosophers through the centuries.

▸ **The basic line of reasoning goes as follows**

- The universe shows evidence of design.

- Designed things have designers.

- Therefore, the universe must have a designer - God.

We can see how this argument is **VALID** - it follows that if the universe shows evidence of design, and designed things have designers, that the universe must have a designer. The soundness of this argument must be established by finding out whether the premises are true. Now, no one will doubt that things that are designed have designers - that's almost **TAUTOLOGICAL** (true by definition) - it's as controversial as saying that pies have pie-makers and dresses have dressmakers. So the soundness of the whole argument hinges on the question of whether the universe shows evidence of design, something about which there has been much ink spilled.

THE INFLUENCE OF ARISTOTLE

Before we move on to look at some more specific teleological arguments formulated over the years, it is important to recognise how Aristotle's thinking about nature has influenced those formulating teleological arguments. Aristotle believed, as you probably know, that each thing in nature has four kinds of explanation. In the modern world, we are most happy explaining something in terms of its origin - how it got there - but

Aristotle recognised that there was more to explaining something's nature than this.

Aristotle said the four explanations were:

1. **MATERIAL CAUSE** - what x is made from

2. **FORMAL CAUSE** - what form x takes (what it is)

3. **EFFICIENT CAUSE** - what made x

4. **FINAL CAUSE** - what x's purpose is

Aristotle thought that purpose was an essential part of fully explaining something's nature, and believed that everything in nature has purpose. This view influenced Aquinas, as we could have predicted, so great was Aristotle's influence on him. It also influenced early writers in Latin, including Cicero, who was one of the first to formulate a coherent teleological argument.

CICERO'S ARGUMENT

> *Is it possible for any man to behold these things, and yet imagine that certain solid and individual bodies move by their natural force and gravitation, and that a world so beautifully adorned was made by their fortuitous concourse? He who believes this may as well believe that if a great quantity of the one-and-twenty letters, composed either of gold or any other matter, were thrown upon the ground, they would fall into such order as legibly to form the Annals of Ennius. (Cicero, De Natura Deorum Book II Chapter 37, trans. CD Yonge)*

Cicero's celebrated work De Natura Deorum (on the Nature of the Gods) was written over 2,000 years ago in the form of a dialogue. In Book 2, Cicero has one of the interlocutors, Balbus, defending Stoic Philosophy, and specifically the idea of the universe having purpose. Here we see quoted the pithiest exposition of this idea. Cicero's argument is clear - the overwhelming likelihood is that the universe has order and purpose not by chance, but by design.

AQUINAS' ARGUMENT

We have said that Aristotle's influence can be seen in the writings of both Cicero and Aquinas. We have examined one; now let us look at the other.

As we know already, Aquinas formulated five "ways" to belief in God. The first three of these ways we examined in the chapter on the cosmological argument. The fourth way we will examine in the chapter on moral arguments later on. It is the fifth of the Five Ways that we are examining here.

> **Aquinas' argument runs as follows**
>
> - Natural objects act towards an end or goal, for a specific purpose.
>
> - We can see this from the fact that they act regularly in order to achieve this purpose.
>
> **Hence their actions are not random but ordered.**

- Now, whatever lacks a mind can't decide to act regularly or with purpose, but must be directed in its action - for example an arrow is shot to its mark by the archer.

Therefore, there must be an intelligent being which directs the movement of natural objects such that they act regularly in achieving their goal. This is what all men know to be God.

You can see the intuitive appeal of what he is saying. Imagine an arrow sitting on a table 200m from a target. It is inconceivable that the arrow **WILL EVER MAKE IT TO THE TARGET ON ITS OWN**; an arrow cannot direct itself towards the bull's-eye.

Aquinas says that all natural objects without minds are like this as their regular, purposive behaviour is directed. How could an apple decide to fall from a tree, in order to allow its seeds to be gathered and moved or the fruit rot and the seeds be propagated that way? Aquinas rightly says that the apple can't choose to fall from the tree. He therefore believes that this directed action requires a director: an intelligent God.

Critics of Aquinas object that since his time scientists have discovered impersonal laws of nature, and it is these physical laws that allow us to understand how natural bodies act regularly.

But Aquinas could easily reply here that he has already said as much in his argument. He has noticed that natural objects without minds act regularly despite the fact that they do not chose to. Laws of nature simply **DESCRIBE** the regularity; they don't explain it.

But there is another viewpoint that we could bring in here to undermine Aquinas' argument. Aquinas' view relies on the assumption that regularity can only be produced intelligently; that something undirected by intelligence will never behave regularly. A long time before Aquinas, however, Epicurus contested that this assumption is in fact not true. According to the Epicurean Hypothesis, as it has come to be known, regularity does not have to come from intelligence, but can emerge from chaos. Imagine you have a pendulum, and you hit it really hard. It will go flying this way and that, chaotically, but eventually it will fall into a regular swinging pattern. In the case of the pendulum, the regularity is not intelligently willed, but emerges naturally out of chaos.

This seems to undermine Aquinas' key assumption, that regularity can only be intelligently directed, not randomly produced, and so we must consider it to be a strong criticism of the Fifth Way.

PALEY'S ARGUMENT

From Aquinas we now fast-forward to 1802, and the publishing of Paley's Natural Theology, in which we find what is now the most famous exposition of the teleological argument. William Paley was a clergyman with a particular interest in the natural world and its apparent order and purposiveness. The argument from design is the foundation of Natural Theology, indeed it is the very first thing he discusses in the book.

Paley gives his argument in the form of an example:

> *In crossing a health ... suppose I ... found a watch upon the ground, and it should be inquired how the watch happened to be in that place; I should hardly think ... the watch might have always been there ... [W]hen we come to inspect the watch, we perceive that its several parts are framed and put together for a purpose, e. g. that they are so formed and adjusted as to*

produce motion, and that motion so regulated as to point out the hour of the day; that, if the different parts had been different ... from what they are ... either no motion at all would have been carried on in the machine, or none which would have answered the use that is now served by it ... The inference, we think, is inevitable, that the watch must have had a maker ... who formed it for the purpose which we find it actually to answer ... and designed its use.

Paley, Natural Theology, 1802

Paley goes on to argue **FROM ANALOGY**, which means using a similar case to argue for a similar conclusion. Paley points out that many natural objects are just as intricately constructed for a purpose as the watch, and so, if we accept that the watch must have a watchmaker, then does it not follow that nature must also have a designer? Take the human eye-ball, for example. It, like the watch is made from little parts (the lens, the iris, the cornea, the retina, the optic nerve) that are perfectly suited to their functions, and which work together to enable sight. Just as we infer a watchmaker from the watch's acting towards a purpose, Paley argues that it follows that we should infer a designer of the world to explain the intricate ordered mechanisms we see in nature.

Like Cicero in De Natura Deorum, here Paley is pointing to the huge improbability of something with order and purpose coming about by accident. Paley is absolutely right that on discovering a watch on a heath, no person would think it had always been there - the little parts that all work together to perform a function suggest that it has been carefully designed. Yet, in this respect, many natural objects also seem to share traits with the watch, so by analogy, Paley is arguing that we should be convinced that the world also is designed.

CONNOR CUNNINGHAM in his excellent BBC documentary **DID DARWIN KILL GOD?** points out something very interesting about Paley's worldview. Paley lived and worked at the beginning of the industrial age, when mechanisation was starting to become much more prevalent. Paley's view of God as a heavenly mechanic, as a maker and tuner of the universe, is therefore very much of its time. Man-made objects are more mechanistic and so parallels between man-made mechanisms and the mechanisms of nature must have been that much more apparent to Paley than perhaps had been the case before. It is not therefore surprising that Paley drew the analogy of the watch and the eyeball.

CRITICISMS OF THE DESIGN ARGUMENT

Hume's Criticisms

The most famous and arguably the most effective of the criticisms against the teleological argument come from David Hume (1711-1776). Hume was a celebrated philosopher and man of letters living at the centre of the so-called Scottish Enlightenment alongside people like the Economist Adam Smith. There is much debate about what Hume thought about religion; many would claim that he was an atheist. After all, many people who followed in his tradition of thinking, that of **EMPIRICISM** (the view that the world is constructed from sense data), were atheists. However, Hume had many friends amongst the clergy and it seems that we can only argue from the evidence that we have that he may have been an agnostic. Still, it is clear that some of Hume's views on religion were thought best to be kept from publication until after his death.

Adam Smith saw that Hume's Dialogues Concerning Natural Religion was published posthumously.

Discussions of this subject often set out Hume's arguments in opposition to those of Paley. But note that Hume was not actually replying to Paley, whose works he never read. He had in fact been dead for 26 years before Natural Theology was published. However, Hume's criticisms undermine some of the key ideas behind all teleological arguments, and hence call Paley's view into question.

So, now let us look at what Hume's critique consists of. Largely, Hume is attacking teleological arguments on the basis that they require the use of **ANALOGY**. They argue that because we know what it is for a human to design, and what sorts of effects design produces, that we can **BY ANALOGY** infer design in the universe as a whole, because of the belief that **LIKE EFFECTS MUST HAVE LIKE CAUSES**. This implies that if x, which is man-made, and y, which is natural, both show evidence of design, then just as x has a designer, so must y.

Now, analogies are best when they are strong, that is to say you are much more likely to be convinced by an analogy if the two things compared are similar, and the more similar the better, because then the comparison will be as strong as it can be. Hume really goes to town on this point, trying to render the analogy so strong that the conclusions are ridiculous. This is a method philosophers call **REDUCTIO AD ABSURDUM**; reducing an argument down to something laughable by working carefully through unforeseen implications of what has been said.

Hume's criticisms are as follows:

▸ **If we are drawing an analogy between human design and divine design, what kind of God does the analogy imply?**

- **A FINITE GOD** - If we are drawing an analogy between human design and divine design, then the divine designer must be like the human designer, hence finite and not infinite. This is an idea of God which is very different from the God of traditional theology.

- **AN ANTHROPOMORPHIC GOD** - In fact, if like effects have like causes then wouldn't this God in fact be human, or human-like? If the analogy is strong, then the divine designer must be very much like a human designer.

- **A DEAD GOD?** - Why assume the designer still lives? There is no evidence that the designer would still need to be alive, as there are many things that have been designed by designers who have since died. There's no reason, according to the analogy therefore to assume that the universe was created by a God who's still around.

- **MANY GODS?** - You would be compelled to ascribe all the work to one designer - wouldn't it be more likely that there were many gods working on such a big project? The world is a big project, and in big human design projects, such as a ship, there are many people working on its design and construction. It seems that if the analogy between human design and divine design is to be strong, there might be many gods working on the design of the world.

▸ **If we are drawing an analogy between human design and divine design, what implications follow from the fact that the universe is imperfect?**

- **AN IMPERFECT GOD / POOR DESIGN** - There seems to be so much that is faulty in the world. Eyesight might seem well-designed, but yet most people end up wearing glasses in middle-age, and some people are born blind. Plants seem to have excellent organs and systems to allow their growth and flourishing, but yet there are diseases that can wipe them out. There is no reason to say that this God is perfect, because there are mistakes and errors found in the design of the universe.

- **A TRAINEE GOD** - In fact, as the world seems to be so full of mistakes, why not infer that this is the work of some trainee God, laughed at by the other gods for the inexperience and naïveté it shows? We can imagine that there could be many worlds, and many much better designed than this one.

▸ **Do we have relevant experience on which to draw analogies about the design of the world?**

- The key supposition in design arguments is that **LIKE CAUSES HAVE LIKE EFFECTS**, but there has only been one universe as far as we know - and we were not there to perceive its creation - it therefore follows that no proper comparison can be made based on empirical evidence, because there is nothing similar enough to the universe to draw a decent comparison.

As we can see, Hume has called into question the whole idea of drawing comparisons between human design and divine design, showing the true implications of saying that like effects have like causes. By drawing a comparison, we do not get to an all-powerful God, but to a finite, anthropomorphic, possibly multiple and probably incompetent deity; hardly the God of classical theism.

However, it is important not to take Hume's critique out of context. Hume's Dialogues Concerning Natural Religion are written, as the title suggests, in the form of dialogues, and none of the characters in the dialogues is called Hume. We cannot therefore be certain which, if any, of the characters is promoting Hume's true view.

The character that strongly contests the validity of arguments from design is Philo, and although his critique is very powerful, he is far from getting the last word in the dialogue as a whole. It is not the vehement critic of religion Philo who wins, but rather the moderate man Cleanthes, who agrees eventually that the argument from design fails, but still believes in God. This is hardly a strong atheist conclusion.

JS MILL

In an essay entitled Nature, JS Mill challenged the idea of nature being designed by an all-powerful and loving creator. Mill points out that it is often wrongly assumed by theologians that the universe is wonderfully fit for our needs, such that it must have been constructed by an intelligent being. This is not at all the case, Mill claims, because when you think about it, mankind has had to constantly manipulate nature, or even work against it in order to meet our needs. Think about it: we need to find or construct shelter and clothing to be warm enough, and we cook food and treat water to ensure that it is safe. We have to know which berries and fungi will nourish us, and which will kill us. In fact, far from reflecting nature's great design, as Paley saw it, you could see pretty much everything man has made or designed as being an improvement on nature. Indeed, as Mill said, if the universe was made by an intelligent being, it can only have been made as a "designedly imperfect work" so that mankind amends it for his own needs.

Mill also thought that a great mistake made by theologians was to assume that goodness was natural; that to act in accordance with nature was correct, and to act against it was bad. Mill pointed out that the worst crimes are almost always committed when man lets his natural, uncivilised tendencies get the better of him. Still, even worse than human nature is nature itself. Even the worst machinations of the human mind cannot outdo nature's cruelty. As Mill said: "Anarchy and the Reign of Terror are overmatched in injustice, ruin, and death, by a hurricane and a pestilence."

Mill sees the cruelty of nature as an insurmountable difficulty for the argument from design, seeing it as impossible for an omnipotent, intelligent designer to have constructed this world.

> *If the maker of the world can [do] all that he will, he wills misery, and there is no escape from the conclusion.*

EVOLUTION

In 1857, a book was published that permanently changed people's perception of the seemingly orderly and purposive way in which the universe seems to run. Charles Darwin's On the Origin of Species claimed that animals and plants were not placed on earth in the way we see them now, but that every living organism evolved from less complex life-forms over many millions of years through a process of natural selection. According to Darwin's theory, what seems to us like a creature fit for purpose, one with organs and systems that work so well towards a goal, is actually a creature fit for survival. Rather than creatures being crafted such that every part of them is evidence of their Creator, living things survive only if their characteristics enable them to. A creature whose traits make them unfit to make it in the environment in which they live will be one that does not survive long enough to reproduce, and hence pass on their traits to their offspring. So, according to Darwin, the reason why the world appears designed is that the living beings, plants and animals, which were not fit for purpose, did not survive, and so they are not here to see.

We can see how this utterly destroys Paley's idea of a Divine Watchmaker, who fashions each little part of creation according to some grand plan. If the theory of evolution is true, then the premise of Paley's argument, that the world shows evidence of intricate design fit for purpose is simply false and his argument fails.

However, when On the Origin of Species was first published, it did not create the uproar that we might expect. Many churchmen accepted it as a good account of how mankind came to be. Even Darwin himself, who did lose his faith, didn't lose it because his view disproved the existence of a designing God, but rather it was the experience of seeing his small daughter get ill, become weak and die that led him to think that there could not be an all-good God. Evolution does undermine belief in Paley's God, a God that designs and sculpts every living thing, but this was not the mainstream view at the time, so evolution was not seen as the challenge to Christianity that it is, perhaps seen as today.

In fact, since Darwin, many philosophers and theologians have attempted to formulate new versions of the teleological argument that do not imply a God who sculpts each part of creation individually, but who nonetheless is the guiding hand behind the structure of the universe.

MODERN TELEOLOGICAL ARGUMENTS

Teilhard de Chardin

Pierre Teilhard de Chardin (1881-1955) was a French Jesuit priest and philosopher who argued that evolution was no reason of itself to argue that the universe has no purpose, and that God is not a guiding hand in creation.

In his celebrated work The Phenomenon of Man, Teilhard de Chardin argued that evolution is purposeful: that evolution is the means by which the world progresses towards perfection, and unity with God. Teilhard de Chardin's idea that creation has to develop into God's likeness is not a new one, but he was unusual in suggesting that evolution is the means by which this perfection is achieved. According to Teilhard de Chardin, evolution is a process by which creatures overcome the need to act only for the purposes of survival, and over time, morality develops. Gradually, creatures become more and more Christ-like, and at the end point (**THE OMEGA POINT** as Teilhard de Chardin called it), perfection is achieved, and the world is united with God.

So Teilhard de Chardin is arguing that God uses evolution **IN ORDER TO ACHIEVE HIS PURPOSE FOR MANKIND**.

However, many have seen flaws in this view. Nature is, as Tennyson said, "red in tooth and claw". For most creatures, and for mankind throughout most of its history, day-to-day life is a battle to survive, a battle to find enough food to live, and to avoid being food to someone else. This hardly seems like the work of an all-loving God. Moreover, if Teilhard de Chardin is right that creation is, through a long process of evolution, eventually going to achieve perfection, then does this not imply that billions of creatures exist only to struggle and die in the process of their successors achieving perfection? Again, this hardly seems to accord with the idea of a benevolent God.

The Aesthetic Argument

FR Tennant in the 20th C responded to the problem of evolution with an appeal to the beauty of the natural world. He claims that although some beauty is needed in the world in order for evolution to function (flowers need to attract pollinating insects; humans need to attract mates etc), there is a superfluity of beauty in the world - there is much more beauty than there needs to be in order for evolution to happen. This suggests, Tennant argues, that there is a benevolent God, who infuses the natural world with beauty purely for His creatures to enjoy.

Many have criticised this view, saying that the beauty of the world cannot be taken as credible evidence for the existence of God. Some say that the idea of the world being beautiful is a selective one. We can all think of absolutely beautiful things to be found in nature, a sunset over a lake, for example - but then what about dog excrement and rotting fruit? These are part of nature too, and yet they don't seem to be infused with beauty.

Others have suggested that beauty in nature might have an indirect benefit for evolution; we might find things beautiful that are of evolutionary benefit. We might find landscapes beautiful because they are places conducive for us to live in; we might find flowers and plants and trees beautiful because they demonstrate that the surrounding environment is fertile and good for food. Just because beauty in nature does not serve a direct benefit in evolutionary terms, it does not mean that it does not have an evolutionary function.

Moreover, beauty is, as Shakespeare said, "in the eye of the beholder", so perhaps humans just have a psychological need to perceive beauty, and whatever we were presented with, we would find beautiful. In a world with no beautiful sunsets, would we find something else equally beautiful? Perhaps there could be a world that was far more beautiful? Imagine if there were a far more beautiful world, and its inhabitants visited our world, would they not conclude that God didn't love our world as much as theirs? Our finding something beautiful is no indication that it is objectively beautiful, and so, many have argued, it cannot be taken as evidence for the existence of God.

The Argument from Fine Tuning

An extremely popular modern teleological argument is the Argument from Fine Tuning. This argument overcomes the challenge of evolution by focussing rather on the overwhelming improbability of any world, and indeed any life existing at all. This argument is widely held amongst those whose work straddles Science and Philosophy or Theology, including such thinkers as the Scientist and Philosopher John Polkinghorne and Physicist Paul Davies.

The argument for the fine-tuning of the universe is as follows: a world in which life is able to be supported is overwhelmingly improbable - there are a number of variables such as gravity, or proximity to the sun which, had they been even slightly different, would have resulted in no life at all. If we were slightly closer to the Sun, or slightly further away from it, there would be no life on Earth. If the temperature at the Big Bang had been ever so slightly higher or lower, no life could have developed. We are Carbon-based life forms, but yet after the big bang, only Hydrogen and Helium existed, and the creation of Carbon was an overwhelming improbability. Paul Davies called this **THE GOLDILOCKS ENIGMA** -

everything in the universe is "just right" for life to emerge on Earth. The probability of everything being absolutely perfectly honed is so improbable that God is a more likely option than its coming into existence by blind chance.

In a way, this takes us back to Cicero's point, that the intricacy of the universe is as likely to come about by chance as throwing all the letters in the air and getting the Annals of Ennius. It is extremely unlikely, and hence we can be persuaded that it cannot be chance, but must be design.

However, this argument is far more plausible when we think of only the Earth because the conditions on Earth are absolutely perfect, so it seems like too much to be coincidence. But doesn't this ignore the fact that we currently know of nowhere else in the universe where life is supported? Physicists claim that the universe is infinite, and in an infinite universe, there is bound to be a place in which life is supported. In most places, the conditions are not right, but here, they are.

You could say that a monkey left to type on his own, would be so unlikely to type the complete works of Shakespeare, that it would not happen, it could never happen by chance. But what if we had infinite monkeys and infinite time? Eventually, it would be bound to happen, however improbable it seems.

But then, advocates of the Argument from Fine Tuning might dispute that this explanation is sufficient. Although given an infinite universe, life somewhere in it is perhaps inevitable, the existence of the universe at all is such an overwhelming improbability, that it seems much more likely that it is down to God's guiding hand.

Advocates of **THE ANTHROPIC PRINCIPLE** claim that any conceivable being would observe their universe and think that it was perfectly fine-tuned for their existence. That is because if it didn't meet their needs, they would never have existed. The seeming fine-tuned-ness of the universe is therefore, on this view, no evidence at all of design, because the fact that we are here to observe the universe means that it is inevitable that it is suited to the kinds of creatures that flourish here. Imagine a world in which Nitrogen, not Carbon-based life forms had evolved. They would look around their world and see how finely tuned their world is for their needs. Of course it is: they wouldn't be there if it weren't.

Ultimately you will be convinced by teleological arguments for the existence of God if you are persuaded that a universe such as this could not come about by chance. If you can conceive that this universe, in all its complexity could and did come about by chance, then you will not find any teleological argument compelling.

KEY TERMS

- **AESTHETIC** - Relating to beauty.

- **ANALOGY** - An example that is similar to the subject about which you are arguing, which is used to argue a point based on a similarity. Analogies are used a lot in teleological arguments.

- **DESIGN QUA PURPOSE** - Teleological arguments can focus on the idea of design in different ways. Some focus on the idea that the universe works in a purposive way, and that purpose implies design. Paley's argument is based on design qua purpose.

- **DESIGN QUA REGULARITY** - Teleological arguments based on the idea that the regular behaviour of natural objects is evidence that they must be designedly like that. Aquinas' teleological argument is based on the idea of design qua regularity.

- **EMPIRICISM** - A philosophical movement that claims that reality is best studied through study of and appeal to sense data.

- **EVOLUTION** - The view that natural objects are not designed, rather that species as a whole develop traits that seem designed because those without useful traits die out, through a process called natural selection.

- **GOLDILOCKS ENIGMA** - Paul Davies' term for the puzzle that the world brings by seeming "just right" in a way that seem overwhelmingly unlikely.

- **LIKE CAUSES HAVE LIKE EFFECTS** - A key assumption

behind many teleological arguments, and the basis on which Hume mounts his reductio ad absurdum.

- **OMEGA POINT** - The end to which evolution is aimed, according to Teilhard de Chardin.

- **REDUCTIO AD ABSURDUM** - An argument that pushes a view to its logical conclusion, in order to show up its flaws.

- **TELEOLOGICAL** - From the Greek "Telos" and "Logos"; reasoning about purpose.

- **TELOS** - Greek: purpose, goal.

SELF-ASSESSMENT QUESTIONS

- On what key assumptions are all teleological arguments based?

- Give at least two examples where analogy is used in a teleological argument to convey the point.

- Give an example of where analogy is used to criticise the teleological argument.

- In what way is evolution a challenge to the thinking behind the teleological argument?

- Was the teleological argument first formulated in the 19th C, 13th C, or prior to that?

- Do teleological arguments necessarily lead to a Christian God? Why/Why not?

- Give five ways in which Hume is successful in his critique of the teleological argument.

- How might you defend Paley's argument against Hume's criticisms?

- How does Teilhard de Chardin attempt to overcome the challenge posed by evolution?

- How might someone criticise the argument from fine-tuning?

FURTHER READING

- **COLE, P** - Philosophy of Religion, Hodder Education, (a number of editions available) Chapter 5

- **DAVIES, B** - An Introduction to The Philosophy of Religion, OUP, Chapter 4

- **JORDAN, LOCKYER AND TATE** - Philosophy of Religion for A level, Nelson Thornes (available in a number of different editions), Chapter 6

- **VARDY, P** - The Puzzle of God, Harper Collins, Chapter 9

The Ontological Argument

The ontological argument is very different from the other arguments we are examining in this book, for a number of reasons. First, it is the only argument we have where its origin seems absolutely clear. It was first formulated by St Anselm of Canterbury (1033-1109) in the Proslogion; there is no evidence that it had been thought of before this.

Secondly, it is different from the other arguments in that it is not an inductive argument, but rather a **DEDUCTIVE ARGUMENT**, one that attempts to draw conclusions based on truths of reason, rather than truths discovered through experience. As we said in the introduction, deductive arguments are potentially stronger than inductive ones, because in an inductive argument the premises are taken from experience and critics can always argue that their experience does not match the premises. In a deductive argument, the premises are truths of reason: they are truths of definition, and so if they are sound and the argument is valid, there is no debate to be had. The conclusion has been proved.

We already know that the "-logical" part of "ontological" means "reasoning" from its appearance in the terms "cosmological" and "teleological". Ontos in Ancient Greek means **BEING**, so the ontological argument is **REASONING ABOUT BEING**. It is based on a discussion of the essential nature of God; what it is to be God.

ST ANSELM

Anselm (1033-1109) was an interesting figure. Born in Aosta, which then would have been on the Burgundian border with Lombardy, he left home in his twenties and entered the Benedictine Abbey in Bec as a novice (trainee monk). He was educated by the renowned Lanfranc, and eventually rose to become Abbot of Bec, and it was here that he wrote his most celebrated works. He was enthroned as Archbishop of Canterbury in 1093. In those days, it was not uncommon to have an Archbishop of Canterbury who was not English as the 16th-C reformation was far in the future. Also, Latin was the language of scholarship, and of the Church, and hence theological and religious institutions could overcome national borders with relative ease.

Anselm's Argument

It could have easily been the case that we never heard Anselm's argument. For a start, Anselm was not much interested in writing, and it was only under the encouragement of his brother monks that he did it. He began writing in his 40s, and although his other works, especially his Monologion and De Veritate were all influential in some way at the time, it is really only for his Proslogion, in which we find his ontological argument, that anyone outside the field of medieval philosophy knows him today.

Anselm's ontological argument itself had a rough ride in draft form. As the story goes, Anselm gave the wax tablet on which he had written the argument to another monk to look after. The monk promptly lost it. Anselm wrote it out again, and then left it for safe-keeping with the same monk (big mistake), who lost it again, and when it was found, the wax was broken into pieces, making the argument indecipherable. To avoid the same thing happening again, Anselm transcribed the argument onto parchment, and hence we are able still to study it today.

The purpose of Anselm's Proslogion is to find unum argumentum - one argument - by which he could prove the existence of God, and from that, everything about God's nature. The ontological argument, which forms the second chapter of the Proslogion is therefore central to the project of the whole book, as it is here that he attempts to demonstrate God's existence.

▸ **Anselm's argument**

1. God is "aliquid quo nihil maius cogitari possit" - that than which no greater can be conceived.

2. This is a definition that even "the Fool that says in his heart there is no God" (Psalm 14:1) would agree with. The "Fool" does not think there is a God, but yet he agrees that this is what we mean by God.

3. This definition of God exists in our minds.

4. It is greater to exist in reality than the mind alone - the painting that a painter produces is greater than his imagining of it before he painted it.

5. But if God (that than which no greater can be conceived) exists only in the mind, then a greater being can be conceived of, namely one that existed in reality as well as the mind.

6. It follows that this would contradict the definition of God as that than which no greater can be conceived.

God must then, in order not to contradict the definition of God, exist in reality as well as in the mind.

Anselm believes that this argument demonstrates that the definition of God implies that he must exist, that to be the greatest conceivable being is to exist. Because existence is, as he says, something that makes something greater, in order to be that than which no greater can be conceived, God must exist.

Having offered his proof for God's existence, Anselm then adds to this argument in Chapter 3 of the Proslogion, arguing that God cannot even be thought not to exist, because a being who can be thought not to exist is not as great as a being which cannot be thought not to exist. This because a being you can imagine not existing is less great than one you can't imagine not existing, so it follows that if God is to be defined as that than which no greater can be thought, then it must be impossible to deny the existence of God.

A contemporary of Anselm's, Gaunilo, who was another monk, is the first known critic of the ontological argument. Gaunilo, despite being a religious man, wrote a reply to Anselm, which he called On Behalf of The Fool, defending the atheist's view that the idea of God does not imply His existence. He uses a **PARODY** of Anselm's argument to show that it is flawed. A parody is a form of **REDUCTIO AD ABSURDUM**, where another version of the argument is given that shows up the flaws in the original argument.

ANSELM'S ONTOLOGICAL ARGUMENT	GAUNILO'S REPLY ON BEHALF OF THE FOOL	ANSELM'S REPLY TO GAUNILO
God is aliquid quo nihil maius cogitari possit – That than which no greater can be conceived.	*Imagine a set of islands that are so great that no greater can be conceived.*	*The parody of the Ontological Argument does not work because the islands are not like God - the very definition of God is that than which no greater can be thought - He is the greatest possible being, not simply the greatest possible x or y. God and islands are not similar cases, so the Ontological Argument has not been successfully parodied.*
This is a definition that even an atheist would agree with.	*These islands exist in our minds.*	
This definition of God exists in our minds	*But it is greater to exist in reality than in the mind alone, so if these islands do not exist in reality, then greater islands can be conceived of, namely islands that exist in reality.*	
It is greater to exist in reality than the mind alone.		
But if God (that than which no greater can be conceived) exists only in the mind, then a greater being can be conceived of.	*So, in order to be the greatest islands conceivable, they must exist in reality as well as the mind.*	
But this would contradict the definition of God as that than which no greater can be conceived.	*But these islands do not, in fact exist in reality, which demonstrates the fact that the reasoning behind this argument does not work.*	
God must then exist in reality as well as in the mind.		

Aquinas' Criticism

Aquinas, as we know already, offered five arguments for the existence of God, but he was deeply opposed to the ontological argument. He believed that the ontological argument is claiming that God's existence is self-evident, which means that it does not need demonstrating. This is perhaps a little unfair on Anselm. He has, as we have seen, given an argument for the existence of God. It seems at first inspection that Aquinas is criticising Anselm for thinking that no argument is necessary. But Aquinas' criticism is not so much that Anselm has no argument as much as it is that he has a deductive argument. All of Aquinas' proofs are inductive; they draw on **EMPIRICAL EVIDENCE**, which Anselm, with his a priori reasoning, does not. When he claims that God's existence is not self-evident, he meant that it cannot be demonstrated using definitions and reason alone; it requires evidence from the world.

DESCARTES' ONTOLOGICAL ARGUMENT

It was generally believed by philosophers and theologians, in the time between Aquinas' criticism of the ontological argument and Descartes' reformulation of it, that Aquinas had provided a convincing challenge, demonstrating that no ontological argument could ever work.

It seems strange then that Descartes (1596-1650) formulated an ontological argument of his own, and in order to properly understand why Descartes chose to revive it, we need first to get to grips with Descartes' general philosophical view.

As you might know, Descartes is best know for employing **SCEPTICISM** as a tool for finding out what can be known for certain. In his Meditations, Descartes asked himself whether he could be sure of the following:

THE THING HE WONDERS IF HE KNOWS FOR CERTAIN	IS IT CERTAIN?
The world as it appears to him at that moment	*It is not certain because he could be dreaming or having a hallucination - there is no guarantee that it is actually there, as sometimes we cannot tell a dreaming state from a waking one.*
The truths of Mathematics	*Maths itself seems to be indubitable (not doubtable), but yet when you do Maths, it's easy to make mistakes and not realise you have, thus making more and more mistakes - with any given mathematical calculation, you cannot be sure that you haven't gone wrong.*
The certainty of anything in the world	*Nothing in the world is certain because there could be some malign demon who is deceiving you on everything, from the nature of the world to the truths of logic and Maths. You could have no body, and just be a mind being manipulated by this demon to think that the world is the way that it seems.*

THE THING HE WONDERS IF HE KNOWS FOR CERTAIN	IS IT CERTAIN?
I exist	**Yes - this is certain.** *It is impossible to doubt the existence of things without existing - doubting requires a doubter. Hence, "I" must exist. In other words I think, therefore I am.*

Having got to the point where he is convinced that he exists, but not that he has a body, or is situated in anything like the world as it appears, Descartes is keen to try to demonstrate that the world is, in fact, how it seems. This is where his ontological argument comes in.

Descartes said that we could know things for certain if we had a "clear and distinct" idea of it, namely a sort of **INNATE IDEA**: something that we cannot doubt even when we try to.

Descartes has said that we could be being deceived by an evil demon that manipulates out minds, but now he wants to argue that this could not be further from the truth. Descartes claimed that we have a clear and distinct idea of a perfect being, God, and formulated the following ontological argument for the existence of this being.

1. I have a clear and distinct idea of a perfect being

2. Existence is part of perfection

This perfect being must, therefore exist.

Descartes uses the example of a triangle. Having three sides and three angles that add up to 180 degrees is essential to the nature of the triangle. If it doesn't have three sides and three angles that add up to

180 degrees, it is not a triangle. Similarly, a perfect being that does not exist would not be perfect, because its existing would be more perfect. Hence, just as you can't remove the three-sidedness from the triangle, you cannot remove the existence from a perfect being.

THIS ...	IS INSEPARABLE FROM
Triangle	*Three sides and three angles*
Mountain	*Valley*
Perfect Being	*Existence*

Another example Descartes employs to make a similar point is that of mountains and valleys. If there is a mountain, there is a valley because it is impossible to have upland without lowland.

From this, Descartes concluded that the supremely perfect being exists, and that He could not be a deceiver, as that would go against the idea of a perfect being. Hence, Descartes concluded that the world as he perceived it was not a deception.

The obvious response to Descartes' view is that there are many people who do not have a "clear and distinct idea" of a perfect being. Perhaps Descartes thought he did, but others don't seem to. Descartes did however foresee this criticism, and claimed that the idea of a perfect being might not be immediately apparent to everyone, but that does not mean that it was not an idea that with careful reflection it would become clear and distinct to them.

Kant's Criticism

The most famous critic of Descartes' formulation of the ontological argument was Immanuel Kant, who as we shall see formulated a moral argument for the existence of God, having rejected the other three arguments.

Kant reacted strongly against the idea that existence can be part of something's essence. He famously claimed that "existence is not a predicate". This means it cannot be part of something's definition to exist. What something is, is one question, and whether or not it exists is another question entirely. You might not be able to deny that three-sidedness is an essential property of the triangle, but you can always deny that there is a triangle as the existence of something is always a separate issue from what its essential nature is.

Existence does not add to something's nature (the function of a "predicate"), Kant claimed, using the example of 50 coins. An imaginary 50 coins and a real 50 coins is not different in value as being real doesn't make it 75 or 100 coins. 50 coins in the mind and in reality are of the same value, and whether it exists in reality is something you do by looking at your bank balance; you can't find it out through deductive reasoning, but only **INDUCTIVELY** through the experience of going to the bank and checking the balance.

However, it could be contested that although it is hard to see how something could exist by definition, there are many things that are non-existent by definition. A square circle cannot exist because it contravenes laws of logic: it is clear that no square circle ever has or ever could exist. No one seems to find any difficulty in saying that part of the essence of a square circle is non-existence. So perhaps existence or non-existence can in fact be part of the realm of definitions, rather than something that must always be established empirically. We do not need to go out on a hunt for a square circle and not claim it doesn't exist until we have searched every inch of the Earth. Moreover, you could say that there are some creatures whose existence is not illogical, but who are defined as being mythical. Unicorns, Centaurs, Griffins are mythical beasts and hence it is part of their definition that they do not exist in the world.

However, this argument is less strong than the example of the square circle, because although unicorns are mythical, if we found one, we would simply change our opinion that the unicorn is mythical. We would not say that the unicorn can't be real. Perhaps this demonstrates that Kant was right that existence and non-existence of beings is something that only could be demonstrated by looking, not through definition.

Modern Formulations

Since Kant's critique of Descartes, new formulations of the ontological argument have steered away from the idea of arguing that existence is part of perfection, and have made use of new philosophical ideas in their arguments. The most famous of the new formulations of the ontological argument are those of Norman Malcolm (1911-1990) and Alvin Plantinga (1932-), both of whom use ideas of impossibility, necessity and possibility in formulating their arguments.

To understand Norman Malcolm's argument, you will need to cast your mind back to the chapter on the cosmological argument, where we discussed contingent and necessary being. To remind you briefly, a contingent being is one whose existence could have been or could not have been. It has two essential properties: it is caused by something else and it is subject to change. A necessary being is one that cannot not exist. An impossible being is one that couldn't exist.

▸ **Norman Malcolm's argument**

- If God exists, he exists necessarily - His existence would never be a contingent matter of fact like our existence - God is not the sort of thing that just could be or could not be.

- God therefore either exists necessarily or He can't exist - his existence is either necessary or impossible.

- God's existence is not impossible.

Therefore, God's existence is necessary.

By denying that God's existence could be like our existence, namely something in the realm of the "could be, could not be", Malcolm has placed God's existence within the realm of "must be" (necessary existence) or "must not be" (impossible existence). God's existence is clearly not impossible, even if some might think it unlikely. So, if you accept Malcolm's premises, he has a valid argument for God's existence.

However, you can argue that Malcolm equivocating (using two senses of a word interchangeably) here. He is using the word "impossible" to mean both a mode of non-existence - ie something that could never be, as well as to mean "inconceivable". He uses the two senses of impossible interchangeably. He is therefore arguing from the fact that God's existence is not inconceivable that it must be necessary, which does not follow logically at all. Let us see what happens when we tidy up his argument to account for this equivocation.

▸ **Modified argument to avoid equivocation**

- If God exists, he exists necessarily - His existence would never be a contingent matter of fact like our existence - God is not the sort of thing that just could be or could not be.

- God therefore either must exist or must not-exist.

- God's existence is not inconceivable.

Therefore, God's existence is necessary.

We can see that this new argument is invalid because the premises don't hang together to form a logical sequence of an argument.

Alvin Plantinga's argument is interesting because it seems we have come full-circle. Of all the post-Anselm arguments, it is the most like Anselm's argument, even defining God in the same way as that than no greater can be conceived, but there is one big change: the use of the modern idea of possible worlds.

In the medieval way of thinking, something was possible if it happened at some point in time, impossible if it never happened, and necessary if it always happened. This makes a great many things that we would want to say are possible, impossible. For example, it is, according to the medieval worldview, impossible that I had one parent who was French, because at no point in time was it or will it be the case that one of my parents is French.

NITROGEN-BASED LIFE FORMS → **FAR WORLD**

A WORLD WHERE ONE OF MY PARENTS IS FRENCH → **NEAR WORLD**

NEAR WORLD

THIS WORLD → **ACTUAL WORLD**

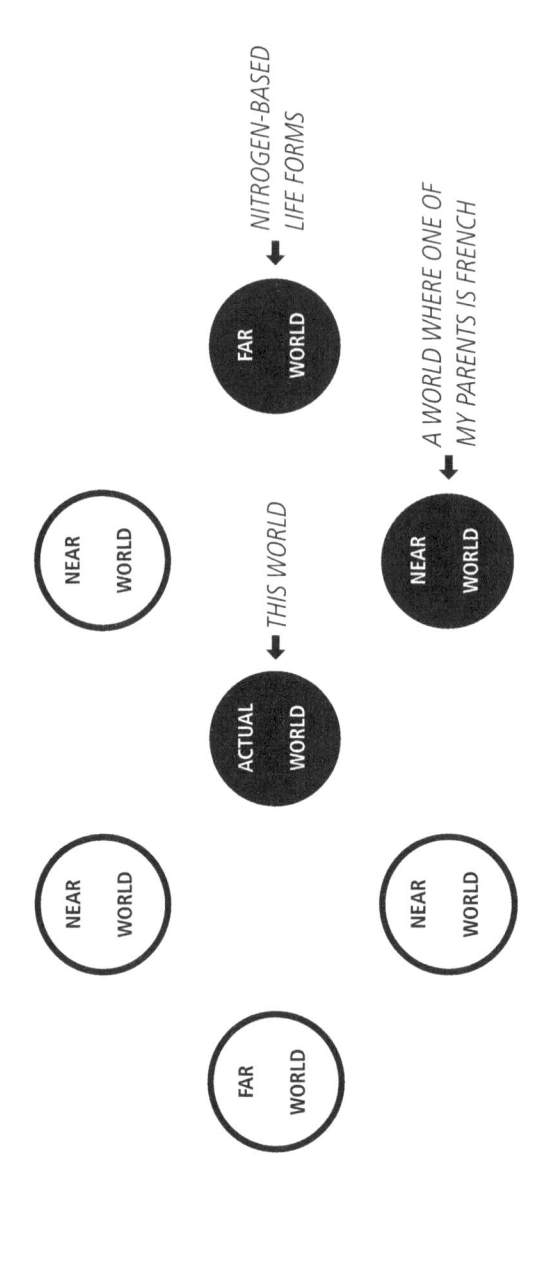

NEAR WORLD

NEAR WORLD

FAR WORLD

NECESSARY: TRUE IN ALL POSSIBLE WORLDS. E.G. 2+2=4

Modern philosophy, on the other hand is much better at talking about what could have been. A "could-have-been" is known as a **COUNTERFACTUAL**. So, it is not the case that one of my parents is French, but it could have been the case that one of them was. Possible worlds are used by modern philosophers to talk about whether something is possible or not. If something is possible, then it exists in some possible world. If it is not possible, it exists in no possible world. If it is necessary, it exists in all possible worlds. There are near and far possible worlds, depending on how like this world they are. I have tried to explain the idea below.

Let us see how the idea of possible worlds plays out in Plantinga's ontological argument.

▸ **Plantinga's ontological argument**

- God is that than which no greater can be conceived.

- God's existence is not impossible; God exists in some possible world.

- But it is greater to exist in all worlds, not just one.

- Therefore, if God is that then which no greater can be thought, then he must exist in all possible worlds, because existing in one world only would contradict his definition as the greatest conceivable being.

Therefore, God exists in all worlds, including this one.

Many philosophers have found this approach interesting, but not convincing. For a start, it assumes that possible worlds must exist - most philosophers use the idea of possible worlds as a tool for talking about what's possible and what's not, rather than believing that these worlds actually exist. For Plantinga's argument to work, there have to be concrete (physically existing) possible worlds.

BETTER TO EXIST IN REALITY?

The Achilles Heel of all ontological arguments, the criticism that simply will not go away, is the idea that it is not better to exist in reality than in the mind. This is arguably key to all ontological arguments.

It is easy to see where the idea of "better in reality" comes from - after all, even though Kant says they are worth the same, if I offered you £50 in your mind or in reality, I think I know which you would take. Real money is so much more useful when you walk into a shop. You try buying that latte with imaginary money.

However, there are also lots of things that you can imagine being worse in reality. I had a dream the other day that an enormous brown bear crashed through my sitting-room window. I was very pleased to wake up and discover that it was not true. It is clear that it is not always better to exist in reality.

This criticism is a real challenge to Descartes' thinking; that existence is part of perfection and that something cannot be perfect if it does not exist. We might think that an imaginary disease or murder would be far better in the mind as something being real does not make it better, so similarly, something does not become more perfect by virtue of existing.

However, this criticism is rather unfairly levied against Anselm. Descartes is talking about perfection, but Anselm never says that it is better to exist in reality. Anselm was careful with his language and his argument, and he does not use the word better ("melius"), but rather he uses the word "maius" (great). In fact, he does not use the word better to describe God until Chapter 5 of the Proslogion - the idea of God being the best conceivable being has no bearing on his ontological argument whatsoever.

Looking at the example he gives of the painter, it is clear he cannot be talking about the idea of existence in reality being better - after all, we all have ideas of what our painting will be, and the reality rarely matches up to the idea. The example of the painter would be a really bad one if he was trying to claim that existence in reality was better. What, I think, Anselm means when he says it is greater to exist in reality rather than in the mind alone is that it is more substantial. A painting is real canvass, and paint and form, not simply an idea because the painting is more substantial than the idea. God is the greatest, the most maximal being there is, and to exist is in this sense greater than existing in in the mind alone.

Anselm's argument still falls foul of Kant's and Aquinas' views that the existence of God is not something that can be established by definition alone, but he is not guilty of thinking God's existence to be better in reality.

FINAL THOUGHTS ON THE ONTOLOGICAL ARGUMENT

Despite many flaws being identified, the ontological argument has neatness and an intuitive appeal. A brilliant story is told (which sadly, is probably not true) about Bertrand Russell, the famous agnostic, seeing the appeal of the argument. Stories differ depending on what source you consult, but he was either cycling down Trinity Street in Cambridge, or walking through a graveyard, and suddenly was struck with a thought:

By Jove! The ontological argument is valid!

In a way, whether this story is true or not doesn't matter, because it shows something that is true about the argument. The reasoning is tight, and intelligent, and although we might finally conclude that it is invalid, it is still an argument with considerable appeal.

KEY TERMS

- **ALIQUID QUO NIHIL MAIUS COGITARI POSSIT** - Latin: Anselm's definition of God - that than which no greater can be conceived.

- **COUNTERFACTUAL** - Something that could have been, according to modern discussions of possibility and necessity.

- **INNATE IDEA** - An idea we are born with - something that is part of the architecture of the mind, and not an idea we acquire.

- **MAIUS** - Latin: "Greater" - the term that Anselm uses in his ontological argument when talking of God.

- **MELIUS** - Latin: "Better" - the term that Anselm uses in Chapter 5 of the Proslogion, but not in his ontological argument when talking of God.

- **PARODY** - A satire - where mimicry is used to show the flaws in an argument - such as in Gaunilo's reply to Anselm.

- **POSSIBLE WORLDS** - A modern way of talking about possibility and necessity, something is possible if there is a possible world in which it is true.

- **PREDICATE** - A quality or property one can say something has, that can meaningfully form a part of the concept of that thing.

- **UNUM ARGUMENTUM** - Latin: One argument - Anselm was trying to find one argument, from which he could infer that God exists, and everything about His nature.

SELF-ASSESSMENT QUESTIONS

- Why is the ontological argument so different from the other arguments for God?

- What was Anselm trying to achieve when he wrote the Proslogion?

- Explain how Anselm's appeal to "the fool" strengthens his argument.

- How does Gaunilo make use of parody to undermine Anselm's argument?

- Aquinas rendered the ontological argument implausible for hundreds of years through making what point?

- According to Descartes, existence is to God as three angles are to triangles, and valleys are to mountains. Why?

- How would Descartes reply if I said I had no innate idea of a perfect being?

- What does Kant mean when he says "existence is not a predicate"?

- Why, according to Plantinga, must God exist in all possible worlds?

- What are the three most problematic criticisms against the ontological argument, in your view?

FURTHER READING

- **COLE, P** - Philosophy of Religion, Hodder Education, (a number of editions available) Chapter 3

- **DAVIES, B** - An Introduction to The Philosophy of Religion, OUP, Chapter 5

- **JORDAN, LOCKYER AND TATE** - Philosophy of Religion for A level, Nelson Thornes (available in a number of different editions), Chapter 4

- **VARDY, P** - The Puzzle of God, Harper Collins, Chapter 8

The Moral Argument

Unlike the other arguments for the existence of God, the moral argument is not so much one argument with a number of versions rather than a series of quite different arguments but with a common theme. We will see later just how different they are from one another. The theme they all share is linking morality with God, and claiming that the existence of morality is evidence, in some sense, for God's existence.

In its simplest form, a moral argument such as this can be given:

▸ **Simple moral argument**

1. If there is objective morality, then there is a God

2. There is objective morality

   Therefore, there is a God.

Moral arguments claim that if there is objective morality (what philosophers call "objective moral facts"), then God is needed, and claiming that there are things that are objectively right and wrong, therefore conclude that God exists. We can see that this simple argument is **VALID**, which is to say that the logic works. We will examine later whether its premises are true or not.

Let us begin by looking briefly at why it might be that God is seen by many as necessary for objective morality.

Why do some see God as being necessary for morality?	→	*God is seen as an omnibenevolent God - a wholly good being, who in the Bible is seen as a lawgiver and judge - where else would morality come from than God?*
But you could say that just because God is defined as being wholly good, it does not follow that there could not still be another explanation for goodness than God.	→	*True, but objective morality seems to be a very strange kind of thing - it requires that goodness is somehow woven into the fabric of creation - that good and bad are inherent in the world, not simply ideas we have constructed - that seems to be something best explained by an appeal to a God.*
But why? Could there not be some other explanation, such as "good is acting for the best interests of others" or "good is something you could will to become a universal maxim"?	→	*But they are ways of describing which acts are good, not what goodness is, or where it comes from. They do nothing to explain why goodness comes from acting in that way. In order to explain goodness itself, an appeal to a God is needed.*

KANT'S ARGUMENT

The thinker most associated with the moral argument is Immanuel Kant. It should be noted though that he probably would not have thought of it as an argument for God's existence. As he says in The Critique of Practical Reasoning Bk II, Ch. II, Section V, (straight after he articulates what we would call his moral argument):

> "... there cannot be a duty to suppose the existence of anything."

Kant does not claim that God's existence has been demonstrated in his work; rather he claims that God is "a postulate of pure practical reason", along with immortality and the freedom of the soul. That is to say that God's existence, an afterlife, and the freedom to choose to be moral are

REQUIRED in order for the idea of a moral order to work; they operate as an **ASSUMPTION**.

In order to understand Kant's view, we need to define a couple of terms from his ethics.

- **GOOD WILL** - A person with Good Will is someone who has altruistic (selfless) intentions, and has the rational capability to work out what the right moral action is. Morality is about selflessly working out the correct action, not about acting in accordance with desires or inclinations.

- **SUMMUM BONUM** - The Summum Bonum is the summit of goodness (literally); it is where the achievement of good is coupled with happiness. The purpose of morality is not for us to be happy, but for us to have earned happiness. A person with Good Will should be able to achieve the Summum Bonum.

It is also important to recognise that Kant thought that the world was fundamentally rational, meaning that moral actions could be derived from reason; in general, the world makes sense.

▸ **Kant's moral argument**

- Everyone with Good Will ought to aim for the Summum Bonum.

- If one ought to achieve the Summum Bonum, there is an implication that it is possible to do so - there is no meaning to saying that one ought to do something that in practice can't be done.

- However, the world is such that we cannot achieve the Summum Bonum in this lifetime - we regularly see the bad prosper and the good suffer. Acting well in this life does not allow us to achieve the Summum Bonum.

- But, as we've seen, we ought to aim for it, which means can achieve it, so if it cannot be achieved in this life, it must be achieved in the next.

- There must, therefore, be an intelligent being who is a guarantor that the Summum Bonum can be achieved in the afterlife.

Kant's argument is not a syllogism as it is not a logical progression of ideas towards an inescapable conclusion. It is more a train of thought; making the case that God's existence is necessary for a moral world view such as his. Because Kant thinks that morality, and more broadly, the world works rationally, the fact that good actions don't lead to happiness doesn't add up. In fact, saying that it doesn't add up is quite a good way of putting it. There is a shortfall between goodness done, and happiness received.

That is why, in Kant's view, an afterlife is needed, as well as a God who can guarantee that being good will lead to the Summum Bonum. This is not an uncommon reason for believing in an afterlife, namely that life can be unfair. Kant's moral argument claims that this is the only solution that can promote a proper moral order.

Criticisms of Kant's Argument

Kant's argument has been quite widely criticised on a number of grounds.

▸ **Ought does not imply can**

Scholars have contested that if one ought to do something, it is not necessarily implied that you can do it. Brian Davies uses the example that, perhaps John ought to learn French, but that is not to say that he can, or certainly that he will ever speak it like a native. JL Mackie further emphasises this in The Miracle of Theism where he claims that even if the fact you ought to do something implies you can go some way to doing it, it does not mean that full achievement of that thing needs to be possible.

We can construct other examples where an obligation does not imply an ability to fulfil that obligation. Imagine John has given up on French, and decides to go out for dinner. When John comes to pay the bill, he finds his wallet has been stolen and so he is both obliged to pay the bill and unable to. Ought, it seems, does not always imply can.

Still, we can see where Kant was coming from; the idea of obligation is based on the assumption that you can do that thing. Imagine John's wallet was not stolen. Then he would recognise that he had an obligation to pay the bill. John would recognise that in ordering from the menu there was an implicit agreement that he would pay for it. That would be a meaningless agreement if John never intended to pay. Similarly, it would be absurd if John said that the fact he ought to pay the bill only means he has to pay for part of it.

▸ The Summum Bonum

The idea of the Summum Bonum is also widely contested. Kant seems to be just asserting that the Summum Bonum exists; that there is a stage at which morality and happiness coincide, but what evidence does he have? Maybe the world is just unfair as maybe the good are not necessarily going to flourish, and the bad sometimes will. Why should it be that the two come together? Psychologically speaking, we might have a strong desire that evil is punished and good is rewarded, but that is not in and of itself an argument to suggest that they must be. We will see later that **FREUD** makes exactly this point.

Kant would argue that to deny the Summum Bonum is to deny the idea that morality is based on rationality. If good does not merit happiness, then morality has no rational basis. Is not morality then reduced to mere inclination to do certain things rather than others?

Moral relativists would argue that morality can be fully explained in just these terms. Morality is just the morals of the individual or group of individuals involved and so there is nothing objective about morality, and reason cannot give you the answer to the question of what should be done. Morality is not, according to them, something present in the world like a law of nature, but more what is custom or acceptable to a certain person or group.

▸ Why God?

Brian Davies criticises Kant's idea that God is the only possible guarantor of the Summum Bonum, saying that some other metaphysical being, such as angels would do just as well. There is no reason why it would have to be a God. However, you could reply in Kant's defence here that angels are said to be spiritual beings created by God, so the idea of there being angels and no God is a little strange. Still, Davies has shown us that one could claim that some rational spiritual being is all that is required, thus meaning God is not a "postulate of pure practical reason".

▸ Rewards for good?

It could be argued that the idea of the Summum Bonum is in tension with Kant's wider ethical scheme. It is extremely important in Kantian Ethics that actions are willed selflessly, and that must be chosen with no hint of inclination: they must be purely reasoned moral choices. Kant would even claim that we should not even consider the needs of our family and friends above others, such is the selflessness of his system.

The idea, then, that morality only works if the good achieve happiness seems to go against this extreme selflessness. Is there not, after all, something in it for you to be good? Kant would claim that happiness is not a reward for good, but something you come to deserve by being good. This does not, however, overcome the tension between the fact that Kant seems to be arguing that goodness should be purely selfless, and that it should also lead to good things for the moral person.

AQUINAS' MORAL ARGUMENT

I said earlier that moral arguments for God's existence have less in common with each other than different formulations of other arguments do. Aquinas' argument (which is the fourth of his Five Ways) takes quite a different tack from Kant's argument, and is based on the idea of a hierarchy of goodness.

> **Aquinas' Fourth Way - (paraphrased for clarity)**
>
> - Aquinas noticed that there are in the world things that are better and worse. Some things are good, and true and just, and other things are less so. From this, as he calls it, "gradation", it follows that there is something that is most good, and that the things that are less good resemble it to a greater or lesser degree. It is just the same with temperature. Hotter things resemble the hottest thing more than the colder things.
>
> - Aquinas then goes on to say that that which is the highest form of x causes the lesser property of x in other things. Imagine we have a fire in the hearth. The fire is the hottest thing in the room, and makes the bricks in the hearth hot, and warms the air, and warms my feet. The hottest thing has caused the heat in all the other things.
>
> - Aquinas then infers that there must be a being of maximal goodness who causes the goodness in everything else. This is God.

Criticisms of Aquinas

- **"Most" does not imply "infinitely"**

Aquinas is absolutely right that if there are different degrees of something, like goodness, present in different entities in the world, it follows that there must be something that is "most good". Here's an example: if I had a series of exam papers to mark, each of which were of different standards, there must be one that is best, out of the papers I have.

However, it does not follow that the best paper I have has full marks. Similarly, it does not follow that the best thing in the world is infinitely good; "most x" is not the same as "entirely x".

Aquinas would think this criticism is missing the point because if the thing that is most good is not entirely good, what does the concept of goodness itself refer to? If we go back to the example of the example of the exam papers, if there were never ever a paper that scored full marks, would the concept of there being full marks mean anything?

- **That which is most x does not always cause x-ness in other things**

Aquinas can also be challenged on the idea that the thing that has most of a quality is the cause of that quality elsewhere. A fire in a hearth is a well-chosen example. It is the fire in the hearth that causes other objects in the room to become hotter, to a greater or lesser extent. Still, not all the heat in the room will be caused by the fire: a lot of my body heat will come from energy released metabolising my food.

But Aquinas is not saying that a fire but fire itself causes all lesser heat, and even in the case of my metabolism this is indirectly true, as it is the heat of the sun that causes things to grow.

However, there are cases where the thing that is most x does not cause x-ness in everything else. Tallness, for example, is a good example of this. The tallest person does not create the height of the less tall people - that seems like nonsense. So Aquinas, (and Aristotle, as this idea comes from the Metaphysics), have been shown to be wrong in supposing that the thing that is most x always is the cause of things that are less x. Hence it can be argued that the most good thing is not necessarily the cause of goodness in everything else.

We have called into question two of Aquinas' major premises: the idea that the thing that is most x is infinitely x, and the idea that the thing that is most x causes the x-ness in other things. We have, therefore made the soundness of Aquinas' Fourth Way very doubtful indeed.

Freud's Alternative Viewpoint on Morality

Freud (1856-1939) is an interesting figure in history, as he is seen to be the originator of both the fields of psychology and the methods of psychotherapy. Freud was the first person, really, to make a study of the mind and its behaviour central to his work. It was he who developed the idea of the unconscious mind, thinking that there are wants and desires that lie beneath the surface. He is famous for using an analysis of patients' dreams in reaching conclusions about their mental states.

Far from thinking that God and morality were inextricably linked, as Kant and Aquinas did, Freud thought that religion was a harmful psychological phenomenon, and that morality was not objective, but was a result of parental and, more broadly, societal expectations. In order to see why this was, we need to examine Freud's understanding of the mind.

Freud's view of the mind is often compared with an iceberg. As we know, what is visible on the surface is just "the tip of the iceberg" as most of it is submerged below water. Freud thought the same was true of the mind. There was far more that lies beneath than that which is presented to the world.

The human mind has three distinct parts, according to Freud:

PART OF MIND	CONSCIOUS/ UNCONSCIOUS	ROLE WITHIN THE MIND
Id	Unconscious	The Pleasure Principle

The Id is the part which drives appetite and self-centred desires. When a child is born, it has no other mode of behaviour apart from the Id, but as it grows up, the demands of the Id are repressed until they become unconscious.

Superego	Largely unconscious, with conscious elements	The Internal Voice of Judgement

The superego develops in early childhood, and is the internalised voice of our parents, issuing us with prescriptions for behaviour. It feels like an objective authority on right and wrong, but it is just the repressive expectations of our parents. The superego conflicts with the Id, and makes a lot of our pleasure-seeking desires unacceptable. Part of the superego remains conscious - we have conscious moral beliefs, but a lot of what we judge our own behaviour and that of others by remains unconscious.

PART OF MIND	CONSCIOUS/ UNCONSCIOUS	ROLE WITHIN THE MIND
Ego	Largely conscious, with unconscious elements	The "ME" you let people see

Ego is the last part to be constructed, and is a balance of the Superego and Id. Ego is the "you" you construct to be acceptable to the world, and it is that that makes up the largest part of your conscious mind.

Freud thought that mental health and wellbeing came of there being a good relationship between these three elements. Neuroses (mental health problems), Freud claimed, often originated in the repression of the Id, and the response that the person has taken to this repression. Because it is parental influence that forms the repressive force of the superego, psychological problems, in Freud's view, often surround the relationship between the child and his/her parents.

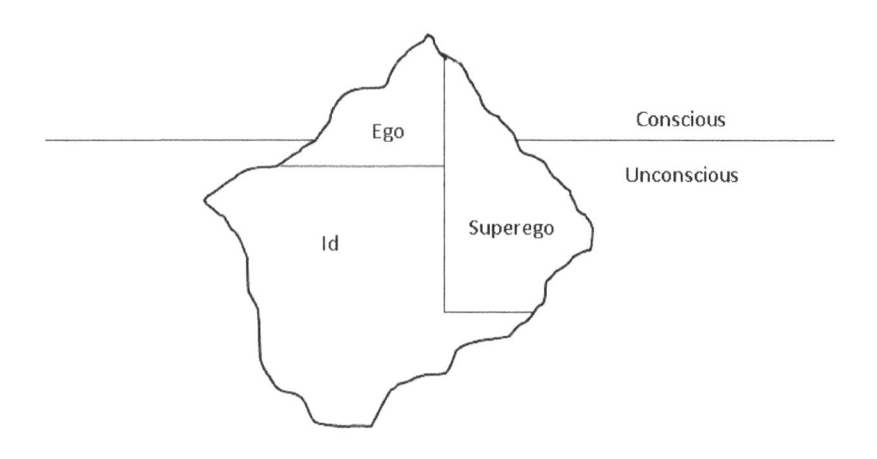

▸ The Oedipus Complex

The myth of King Oedipus is used by Freud as a metaphor for the repression of the Id that happens in early childhood.

Oedipus was born to King Laius and Queen Jocasta. When Oedipus was young, the Oracle at Delphi prophesied that Oedipus would kill his father and marry his mother. The Oracle was never wrong, and so King Laius abandoned his son on a hillside. Oedipus was found and raised by another King and Queen. As a young man heard the prophecy himself. Thinking that he was destined to kill the King he thought to be his father, and marry the woman he thought was his mother, Oedipus ran away over the hills. As he made his way to Thebes, he met an older man in a chariot coming the other way. The two quarrelled about who should give way, and eventually, Oedipus killed the older man. He got to Thebes, finds that the King, Laius, had recently died. He fell in love with Queen Jocasta, and they married and have children. Eventually, Oedipus found out that it was he who killed King Laius, and gradually he put the pieces together, coming to the awful realisation that the prophecy, in all its dreadfulness, had come true. In self-disgust, he blinded himself.

Young children, Freud claimed, have a desire to possess their mothers and kill their fathers. Freud is extremely unorthodox in this view as he did not think that children were sexually innocent; rather he thought that the infant is a bundle of appetites, including sexual desires, which are then repressed in early childhood.

The father is a rival for the mother's love and attention, and is therefore a threat to the child. The father is also strong. The child comes to realise that it has no hope of possessing the mother and getting rid of the father. The child develops a complex feeling of hatred, fear and respect for the father, and learns over a period of years to disguise the desire for the mother and hatred for the father, until these feelings are totally repressed. They become completely unconscious.

Freud called this phenomenon the Oedipus complex, and used it as an explanation for a lot of adult mental health problems (or, as he called them, neurosis). Unhealthy mental states are, according to Freud, usually derived from unresolved issues surrounding our relationships with our parents, and indeed, in a healthy adult, these unresolved issues can be at the centre of our deepest worries and insecurities.

Freud and Religion

Famously, Freud claimed that religion was a neurosis; a mental illness. He called religion a "universal obsessional ritual", and claimed that not only was it untrue, it was harmful.

▸ **Religion enables us to deal with the Oedipus Complex**

At its core, the Oedipus Complex boils down to issues surrounding guilt for desiring the mother, and mixed feelings of fear and respect towards the father.

Religion allows people to feel they can overcome this guilt through ritualistic behaviour, which soothes psychological distress. Deeply-felt emotions of unworthiness, or the feeling of being "sinful", can be overcome through prayer and other rituals.

As we grow older, our own father seems all too human; not the omnipotent being that struck fear into our hearts as infants. Religion provides a heavenly father, God, who is able to command both the fear and respect created towards the father in early childhood.

God is a figure that can make demands and requirements of our behaviour, acting as the arbiter of Good and Evil, just as our father did in our infancy.

▸ **Religion allows us to work through traumas in the evolutionary past**

Freud thought that religion is not just a psychological soother for our individual pasts, but for our collective past.

Freud claimed that current religious practice is likely to be informed by the psychological phenomena found in primal societies.

In is view of the Primal Horde, Freud suggests that there was an alpha male, who alone had access to the females of the tribe. This alpha male would have been respected and feared, but eventually may have been killed out of jealousy by the other males. This resulted in a tremendous guilt, and the tribe therefore erected a totem to both bring back and represent the alpha male.

Freud claimed that it was this that was the first creation of a God, and that the practice has continued as a way of soothing a collective unconscious.

▸ **Religion allows us to work through traumas in the evolutionary past**

Freud thought that religion is not just a psychological soother for our individual pasts, but for our collective past.

Freud claimed that current religious practice is likely to be informed by the psychological phenomena found in primal societies.

In is view of the Primal Horde, Freud suggests that there was an alpha male, who alone had access to the females of the tribe. This alpha male would have been respected and feared, but eventually may have been killed out of jealousy by the other males. This resulted in a tremendous guilt, and the tribe therefore erected a totem to both bring back and represent the alpha male.

Freud claimed that it was this that was the first creation of a God, and that the practice has continued as a way of soothing a collective unconscious.

Kant and Freud

You can see that Freud's view on religion was very different from Kant's. Whereas Kant sees God as the necessary basis for rational objective morality, Freud sees God as a psychological creation by mankind that fulfils our deep-seated desire for an objective standard of goodness; for justice, sense and purpose in our lives.

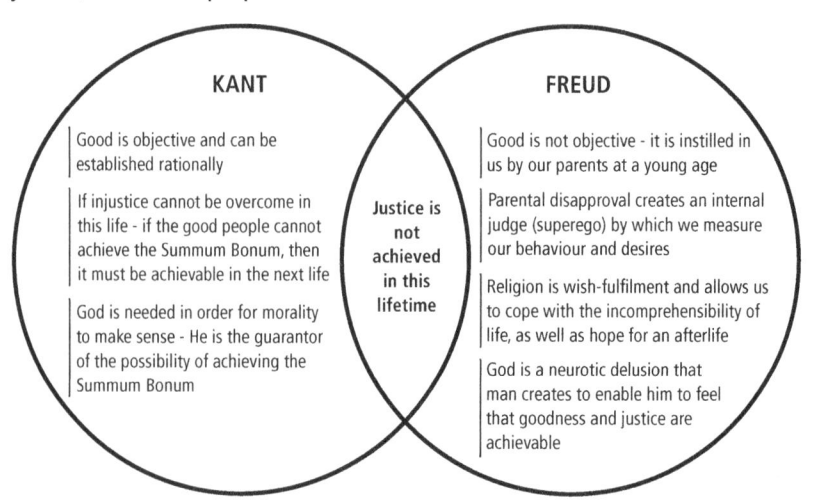

KANT

- Good is objective and can be established rationally
- If injustice cannot be overcome in this life - if the good people cannot achieve the Summum Bonum, then it must be achievable in the next life
- God is needed in order for morality to make sense - He is the guarantor of the possibility of achieving the Summum Bonum

Justice is not achieved in this lifetime

FREUD

- Good is not objective - it is instilled in us by our parents at a young age
- Parental disapproval creates an internal judge (superego) by which we measure our behaviour and desires
- Religion is wish-fulfilment and allows us to cope with the incomprehensibility of life, as well as hope for an afterlife
- God is a neurotic delusion that man creates to enable him to feel that goodness and justice are achievable

Freud would claim that Kant's argument is based on nothing but wish-fulfilment; that Kant wishes that it were the case that good people can achieve the Summum Bonum in an afterlife governed by God. However, wishing something were so is not the same as demonstrating it is the case.

Freud thought that religion was a tragic mental illness:

> "The whole thing is so patently infantile, so foreign to reality, that to anyone with a friendly attitude to humanity it is painful to think that the majority of mortals will never be able to rise above this view of life." Civilization and its Discontents, 1930

Criticisms of Freud's viewpoint

Freud's viewpoint has been extremely influential on society, with his ideas affecting not just how mental illness is viewed and treated, but also how we perceived our minds, ourselves and our desires. Freudian thinking has even influenced the way in which things like advertising work, by appealing to our deepest desires, rather than just telling customers about how good the product is. Freudian analysis became popular and influential, but now is embedded in how people think of human behaviour.

However, Freud's views have also been widely criticised. Let us examine which aspects are more an less controversial:

▸ **Less controversial**

- Not all our mental states are necessarily conscious.

- We can have unconscious desires which can affect our conscious actions.

- Trauma in childhood can result in neurosis in adulthood.

- Morality is, at least in part, transmitted to us by our parents.

▸ **Controversial**

- All infants suffer the trauma of the Oedipus Complex.

- Religion is wish-fulfilment.

- Religion developed from the primal horde.

- Religion is a neurosis.

Let us look at some of the more controversial aspects of Freud's viewpoint:

▸ **All infants suffer the trauma of the Oedipus Complex**

The idea of the Oedipus Complex is one of the most controversial, and indeed ridiculed of Freud's theories. There is, many claim, no evidence at all that we suffer this trauma - when it is first explained to us, it hardly seems to ring true that we have sexual desire our mothers and want to kill our fathers.

Freud would of course contest that it wouldn't seem likely to us, because these are not conscious but unconscious desires. We would only be aware of them if they were conscious. Moreover, the fact that the idea of wanting to sleep with our mothers and kill our fathers is so utterly repulsive to us is further evidence of the repression of these feelings as the superego responds strongly against the very idea of such a thing.

Ultimately, The Oedipus Complex is **UNFALSIFIABLE**. You cannot show it to be wrong, because by its very nature as a repressed trauma there would be no evidence for it. However, the fact that it cannot be shown to be incorrect is not evidence that it is correct, and many would claim that Freud offered too little evidence to convince us of this universal infantile neurosis.

▸ **Religion is wish-fulfilment**

Many have also criticised Freud's claim that religion is wish-fulfilment. On the face of it, Freud's account seems to have some credibility to it because religion does seem to conveniently address some of our deepest wishes, for example, that life is fair and that justice is done; that there is more to life than the daily humdrum existence that most of us lead; that there is someone who will utterly and unconditionally care for us; that there are objective moral standards to live up to.

However, Freud's view is limited here for two reasons. Firstly, just because something fulfils a wish, it does not mean that it is not true. For example, I might have a wish for a sandwich. If something fulfils that wish, namely eating a sandwich, it doesn't follow that, because it fulfils my wish, the sandwich is not really there. In fact, the fact that my desire has been fulfilled, in the case of the sandwich, is probably good evidence that it is real. **CS LEWIS** (1898-1963) made a similar point in his argument from desire - desiring something implies the existence of that thing. I can't desire a sandwich unless sandwiches exist, and so you could argue that desiring God implies that God exists (there are flaws with this view, but we won't get diverted here).

Secondly, Freud is employing a method called **REDUCTIONISM** to religion, which is when you try to analyse something's true nature by reducing it down to its most basic explanation. Many could argue against this, saying that even if religion fulfils wishes, it does not mean that **THIS IS ALL IT IS**. Religion might always involve wish-fulfilment, but then again, eating a sandwich always involves hunger being satisfied . This does not mean that there's nothing else to it, like nourishment, taste, digestion, increased blood-sugar levels, and many other things as well.

▸ **Religion can be explained as having an origin in a collective unconscious - such as the Primal Horde**

This is often taken to be one of Freud's weakest arguments against religion. He gives no real evidence that this Primal Horde ever existed - indeed it is just a suggestion of what could have been the case. It is true that his explanation of the Primal Horde could be true, but then Freud has not demonstrated it.

Freud's supposition that the creation of God was down to the killing of the alpha male, and making a totem to him out of guilt, it therefore mere assertion, and hence there is no real reason to take his view particularly seriously.

Some have accused Freud of creating his story of the Primal Horde to fit the phenomena he saw in Christianity. He even tells a tale of how it could have been that the alpha male was killed and eaten by the other males in the tribe, and this guilt became ritualised in something that has become the communion ritual of Christianity. Again, Freud offers no evidence that this really was the case.

Moreover, even if it were true, (and as we have said, there is very little evidence for this), Freud is committing the **GENETIC FALLACY** here, which is when you claim that because something has a certain origin, the origin is enough to explain it in its entirety. Just because you began life as a fertilised egg, it doesn't mean that that's what you really are now. Even if there was once a tribe that killed and ate its alpha male, and this was the ultimate origin of the communion ritual of Christianity, (and that's a big if), that would not mean that the idea of communion all boils down to that.

▸ Religion as a Neurosis

Life is hard, and full of challenges that we have to work our way through and overcome. Freud thought that religion was a harmful delusion that allows us to sooth our troubled minds with rituals and the belief in a supernatural father who will make everything come right in the end. This, Freud saw as a way of ignoring the profound psychological issues that lie at the heart of this behaviour.

Many would accept that this might be the case for some religious believers; that ritual can become a psychological soother, but that does not mean that this is the case in all religious practice. Ritual is understood as an act of devotion, not a method of soothing a troubled soul.

Freud might argue that devotion to God is in itself troubled behaviour, and it might seem to some that the fact that believers call God "Father" is indicative of the Oedipus Complex affecting religious belief. The question of how religious language works, however, is a very contentious issue; the word "Father" is, according to Aquinas, used **ANALOGICALLY** as an analogy for how to relate to God, not **UNIVOCALLY** which would imply that Christians are trying to create father idols. No, instead of this Christians are trying to find language to best describe what God means for humanity. Freud could, however respond here that even using analogical language, the fact that "father" seems the most appropriate term for addressing God is psychologically dubious.

Freud - Final Thoughts

Although Freud's views on religion seem to have some real appeal in offering psychological explanations for various religious phenomena, Freud's evidence for his claims is thin at best, and often he offers no justification whatsoever. We can only conclude that if Freud is right about religion, he has not sufficiently demonstrated that he is.

TWO GENERAL CRITICISMS OF MORAL ARGUMENTS

Bertrand Russell

Bertrand Russell's criticism of the moral argument centres around the premise that only if you have God, can you really have morality. Russell undermined this point by arguing that far from being the only explanation of morality, religion is on the contrary responsible for a huge amount of violence and evil that goes on in the world. Russell concluded that it was hardly obvious that God and good go together.

It is true that a huge number of conflicts over the years have had religion at their centre. From the crusades to 9/11, religion always has, and still does lead to bitter fighting and violence. In many of the historically most troubled spots in the world, Northern Island, The Middle East, the Pakistan/Indian border, religion is a key aspect of conflict. When people fight over religion they fight over principles, and wars such as these can be much harder to resolve than other conflicts.

However, just because wars have been fought and atrocities have been committed in the name of religion, it does not follow that religion does prescribe this behaviour, and it certainly does not follow that the acts of religious believers negate the possibility of a wholly good God who establishes moral order.

JL Mackie - Argument from Queerness

JL Mackie (1917-1981), in his much-celebrated work Ethics: Inventing Right and Wrong, undermined the idea of objective moral facts, using what he called "the argument from queerness". He begins the book with the phrase "There are no objective values."

He did, however, agree with many theists that if there were objective morality, it would require a supernatural explanation. He famously said that without a God or a similar being, objective morality would be metaphysically queer, which means that they would be a strange sort of thing to exist.

> "The objectivist may have recourse to ... God: the true purpose of human life is fixed by what God intended (or, intends) men to do and be ... God made men for this end and made them such as to pursue it ... I concede that if the requisite theological doctrine could be defended, a kind of objective ethical prescriptivity could thus be introduced. Since I think theism cannot be defended, I do not regard this as any threat to my argument." Ethics: Inventing Right and Wrong, JL Mackie, 1977

By looking at the comparison below, you can see how exactly a simple formulation of the moral argument, and JL Mackie can have same starting point but lead to very different conclusions.

▸ **Simple Moral Argument**

- If there is objective morality, then there is a God.
- There is objective morality.
- Therefore there is a God.

▸ **JL Mackie's Argument**

- If there is objective morality, then there is a God/supernatural explanation - otherwise it would be too strange a thing to exist.
- There is no God.
- Therefore, there is no objective morality as it would be "metaphysically queer".

Mackie's argument against objective values has highlighted one key point - premise 1 only leads to God if you already are convinced of objective moral facts.

Final Thoughts on the Moral Argument

Perhaps the moral argument, and JL Mackie, too, have highlighted for us the fact that objective moral facts are hard to argue for without an appeal to a supernatural entity; goodness as a natural phenomenon in the world does seem like a strange thing to exist; even a metaphysically queer thing to exist. However, what has not been demonstrated is that morality is objective: there may, as Freud noted, be considerable appeal in believing in justice and goodness as objective qualities, but the appeal of objective morality does not, in and of itself, make it more likely.

KEY TERMS

- **POSTULATE OF PURE PRACTICAL REASON** - Kant thought God was needed for morality to function - God is a postulate (something required) of practical reason (moral reasoning).

- **EGO** - In Freud's view of the mind, the part of the mind that is mainly conscious, and is the part of you that you allow the world to see - an acceptable construct.

- **GOOD WILL** - A person with Good Will is someone who has altruistic (selfless) intentions, and has the rational capability to work out what the right moral action is.

- **GRADATION** - Hierarchy - Aquinas argues for God on the basis of "the natural gradation" found in nature.

- **ID** - In Freud's view of the mind, the part of the mind that children are born with, but is largely suppressed in infancy. It is the pleasure-principle.

- **METAPHYSICALLY QUEER** - JL Mackie's term explaining why morality would be odd without God.

- **NEUROSIS** - Freud's term for a mental illness or disturbance.

- **OEDIPUS COMPLEX** - Freud's view that everyone has a repressed desire to kill their fathers and marry their mothers, on which a lot of psychological problems relating to how we deal with authority stem.

- **PRIMAL HORDE** - Freud's idea of a primitive religion, in which he explores possible psychological origins behind certain religious behaviours, including eucharist.

- **SUMMUM BONUM** - The Summum Bonum is the summit of goodness (literally); it is where the achievement of good is coupled with happiness.

- **SUPEREGO** - In Freud's view of the mind, the part of the mind where morality is dictated. It is formed in early childhood, and is the internalised voice of parental and societal prescriptions for behaviour.

- **UNCONSCIOUS** - Psychological phenomena of which the person is unaware - an idea that was pioneered by Freud.

- **WISH-FULFILMENT** - Freud thought that religion just fulfilled psychological needs.

SELF-ASSESSMENT QUESTIONS

- For what reasons do many people claim that God and morality go hand in hand?

- Why is it a problem for Kant that the Summum Bonum cannot be achieved in this life time?

- Name and explain the basis for the three postulates of practical reasoning, according to Kant.

- Why does Kant think that "ought" implies can"? What criticisms can be given of this view?

- Why does Aquinas argue for an infinitely good God?

- What arguments might you give to undermine his argument?

- For what psychological reasons might you believe in God, according to Freud?

- What basic viewpoint do Freud and Kant share? Give three ways in which they infer different things from that basic starting point.

- How could you respond to Russell's criticism that religion is often associated with violence?

- Do you agree with JL Mackie that objective morality cannot be established without God?

FURTHER READING

- **COLE, P** - Philosophy of Religion, Hodder Education, (a number of editions available) Chapter 6

- **DAVIES, B** - An Introduction to The Philosophy of Religion, OUP, Chapter 12

- **JORDAN, LOCKYER AND TATE** - Philosophy of Religion for A level, Nelson Thornes (available in a number of different editions), Chapter 7

Postscript

Clare Jarmy read Philosophy at St Catharine's College Cambridge, before training to be a teacher. She is Head of Philosophy and Religious Studies at Bedales School in Hampshire.

With thanks to everyone at PushMe Press and Ian Douglas for their help at the editing stage.

Students seeking fuller explanations and a bibliography should also consult the website which also contains exam tips and past questions listed by theme.